HIKE SMART

HIKE SMART

Tips and Tactics for Improving Your Treks

Ann Marie Brown and
Terra Breeden

Skyhorse Publishing

Skyhorse Publishing books may be purchased in bulk at special discounts for sales promotion, corporate gifts, fund-raising, or educational purposes. Special editions can also be created to specifications. For details, contact the Special Sales Department, Skyhorse Publishing, 307 West 36th Street, 11th Floor, New York, NY 10018 or info@skyhorsepublishing.com.

Skyhorse® and Skyhorse Publishing® are registered trademarks of Skyhorse Publishing, Inc.®, a Delaware corporation.

Visit our website at www.skyhorsepublishing.com.

10 9 8 7 6 5 4 3 2 1

Library of Congress Cataloging-in-Publication Data is available on file.

Cover design by Tom Lau
Cover photo by Ann Marie Brown
All photos by Ann Marie Brown

Print ISBN: 978-1-5107-0851-8
Ebook ISBN: 978-1-5107-0852-5

Printed in China

Table of Contents

Acknowledgments

We'd like to thank the many people who offered up their hiking and adventure stories for this book. All the people we interviewed were incredibly generous with their time, insights, and honesty. Many of them are our long-time friends; others were strangers before this book was written but have since become friends. The list includes Laura Van Antwerp, Mason Brutschy, Stephanie Coates, Maralana Fulton, Brian Gass, Rosie Hackett, John Kleinfelter, Harriot Manley, Kip Myers, Erica Nelson, David Orr, Adam Peters, Richard Platt and his son John Platt, Suzanne Roberts, Jack Scheifly, Scout Sorcic, Kerri Stevenson, Kim Wyatt, and Katie Zanto.

We'd also like to offer a special thank you to the search-and-rescue professionals who spent many hours offering up their knowledge and expertise, answering pesky questions, and patiently explaining their fascinating work. These people had a lot more important things to do than talk to us, and yet they willingly put those things aside for this book. A huge thank you goes out to Michael St. John and Bob Gehlen of Marin County Sheriff's Office Search and Rescue, John Platt of Valley Search and Rescue, and Lisa Whatford and Chris Kozlowski of El Dorado County Search and Rescue. Thank you for all that you do.

Introduction

Each year, thousands of hikers and backpackers have wonderful trips in America's backcountry. They rejuvenate their souls and find relief from the noise, crowds, and hectic pace of our urbanized lives, all while reveling in nature's beauty.

Every year, however, hikers experience mishaps in the outdoors. These range from the mildly uncomfortable—like not having enough snacks or getting blisters on your feet—to moderately scary—like getting lost or running out of water. Sometimes relatively small problems escalate to become downright disasters, like when hikers get injured or become so disoriented that they can't find their way out.

In the course of writing this book, we found that even the most experienced hikers—including search-and-rescue professionals, outdoor leadership instructors, and backcountry guides—had a wealth of tales about the errors they made (and learned from). It became clear to us that even trail-hardy experts are often just one misstep away from having their photo appear on the evening news.

Fortunately, every mistake that someone makes on the trail gives the rest of us a chance not to fall victim to that same error. We can learn from each other, improve our skills, and get smarter. And that's what this book is about. It includes lots of tips and techniques for better hiking trips, but perhaps more importantly, it details the personal narratives of people who made a wrong turn or committed an unfortunate error, but ultimately learned a valuable lesson in the process.

It would seem dishonest to leave out my own (Ann Marie's) hiking mishap from this book, so here goes: In 2001, I was on a solo road trip, traveling around and hiking different trails every day. When I was on the trail, I carried a full pack with all the hiking essentials as well as a few extras, like a cell phone, extra clothing, and some basic first aid supplies.

One afternoon, I walked about four miles from my car. My trail reached a stream crossing about three feet wide. I jumped across—a simple movement I had executed hundreds of times before—but when I landed on the far side, my right foot slipped on wet granite, and my ankle twisted around as I fell. As soon as I hit the ground, I felt a sharp pain and thought, *I just broke bones.*

The pain was severe enough to make me dizzy, but I was sitting just inches from the creek, so I reached my hands into the cold water and splashed my face. *Don't faint*, I ordered myself. It seemed critically important that I stay focused.

I took off my hiking boot and assessed my ankle. It wasn't pretty. I felt the urge to faint again, so I splashed more cold water on my face, then reached for one of my hiking poles and tried to use it to stand up. It was immediately clear that my right leg could not bear any weight. This was bad.

I pulled out my cell phone and turned it on, but there was no signal.

I decided to rest a while and try to regain my mental equilibrium. I ate a snack from my pack and drank some water. I assessed my situation: Since I was road-tripping, no one knew exactly where I was, or that I had gone hiking that day. I was on a trail that was not frequently used; in fact, on my hike in I had noticed how overgrown the vegetation was. In some places, it almost covered the trail. My car was parked alongside the road, but this was a seldom traveled country road. It might take a while before someone noticed that a blue Toyota hadn't moved in a few days.

It was mid-afternoon, and I had a few good hours of daylight left. My pack had enough supplies in it so that I could spend the night without risk of hypothermia, but it would be an uncomfortable night. My ankle was getting bigger and uglier by the minute.

I added it all up and figured that since no one was coming to rescue me, I might as well try to get back to my car. Walking was out, so I'd have to crawl. I wrapped some extra clothing around my knees and hands for protection and gave it a shot.

Until you've tried it, you can't understand how inefficient crawling is. It takes what seems like forever to go 100 yards. It's exhausting, too, especially for your back and arms. So you stop and rest a while. You check your cell phone again to see if you've miraculously gotten a signal, and then you crawl another 100 yards. In an hour or two, the clothing that you've wrapped around your hands and knees is shredded and torn, no longer protecting you from the rocky trail.

So it went for a couple of hours, at which point I had traveled maybe a half mile. I still had a long way to go, but I told myself I'd go another half mile and then stop and sleep for the night. I had a Mylar emergency sleeping bag, and I trusted its insulating properties to keep me alive. I even had some naproxen in my pack, which would work as a bedtime painkiller.

I'd like to say that I was feeling mentally tough, and that I knew I would get out of there safely. But I was feeling stupid. I was mentally kicking myself for going on this hike without telling anyone, without even leaving a note in my car. I had made a rookie error, and I wasn't even a rookie. I was also mad at myself for being "clumsy" and falling. And I was a little worried about wildlife—I knew this was prime mountain lion territory, and I was pretty sure I had spotted tracks in the mud by the creek.

Dusk was falling, and I was resting from another 100-yard crawl when a miracle happened. Two young men walked around a bend in the trail. "Hey!" I yelled. "I need your help." They spotted my grotesque ankle and my cut-up knees and said, "Ugh, what happened?"

Neither man looked older than twenty. One was covered with tattoos; the other seemed to be under the influence of something, but I was in no position to be picky about who rescued me.

What came next was a comedy of errors as we tried to figure how they could carry me out. First I put one arm around each of their necks, and I tried to hop on one leg. That was slower and more exhausting than crawling. Then they tried to make a litter, but that didn't work. I suggested that one of them run back to the road and go for help. But suddenly the tattooed guy, Rick, said, "Wait, let me do this," and he lifted all 130 pounds of me on to his back. I was astonished. His friend was astonished. But off we went.

Rick had to set me down every 100 yards or so, and when we stopped, he talked. He told me how his parents had kicked him out of the house when he was sixteen, and how he had just been released from juvenile prison for stealing a car—but it wasn't his fault.

He may have been an unlikely savior, but in a couple of hours we were back at my car, and soon, I was riding in an ambulance.

This story has a postscript. When I got back home, I had surgery on my ankle. The doctor reassembled it with six titanium pins and a plate the size of a credit card, and I was sentenced to several long, boring weeks on crutches. A few days into my recovery, I found a piece of paper on which I had scribbled the address of my rescuer Rick. I put a few hundred bucks into an envelope and wrote this note:

Dear Rick,

If you ever find yourself wondering if your life really matters, or if you've done something good that made a difference, let me assure you that you have. You were the stranger who carried me on your back. I am forever grateful.

I never heard back from Rick, so I don't know if that letter reached him or what became of his young and apparently troubled life. Maybe that's inconsequential. I'm sure he knew that he rescued me, and I like to think that this event positively influenced his life, as it did mine.

Ann Marie Brown, January 2017

1
Risk and Rescue

Hikers and backpackers who need to be rescued from the wilderness invariably say they never expected to run into trouble. They assumed that a disaster couldn't or wouldn't happen to them, or, if it did, they would somehow figure a way out of it. Typically they didn't consider all of the possible risks involved. They didn't plan ahead for factors they couldn't control, and they didn't have a contingency plan—or think they needed one.

It seems that part of what makes us human is our belief that everything is going to turn out fine, especially if we're headed for outdoor fun or vacation time. And yet, the National Park Service alone spends nearly $5 million a year on search-and-rescues, and that figure doesn't account for the hundreds of thousands of volunteer hours that go into those searches. National parks are only a tiny fraction of the public lands that Americans use for recreation, so this accounts for only a tiny fraction of total rescues.

Outside of national parks, search-and-rescue operations are typically run by a county sheriff's office. It's the job of these search-and-rescue crews to save our butts when we make mistakes—and the vast majority of them do it on a strictly volunteer basis. Given that, we wanted to hear their perspectives on risk and rescue.

Marin County Search and Rescue prepares for a rescue on a steep cliff in Point Reyes National Seashore.

The Swiss Cheese Model of Failure

Michael St. John is the kind of super-fit fifty-two-year-old who rides his mountain bike around town instead of driving. His day job is Battalion Chief for the Mill Valley Fire Department, but he's even more devoted to his volunteer job as a Unit Leader for the Marin County Sheriff's Office Search and Rescue Team. In his backyard in Fairfax, California, Michael's tricked-out camper truck is packed and ready, so when hikers go missing, he can go find them.

"Wilderness is good for us," Michael says. "Far more good comes from wilderness than harm. But there's some level of risk that people have to accept and take on."

Michael's been working in search-and-rescue since 1980. Since that time, he has participated in hundreds of searches for missing hikers. He says that managing your risk level in the outdoors is important for everybody, whether novice or expert.

Search and rescue teams utilize military helicopters to access hard-to-reach mountainous terrain.

"You could be the most highly qualified mountaineer or hiker, and you simply roll your ankle and fall off a cliff. There are always unforeseen things," he says.

He points to James Reason's Swiss Cheese Model of Accident Correlation, a model for dissecting the anatomy of an accident or error. It's based on the theory that there's never just one factor that causes a serious problem—it's the accumulation of several factors.

Michael says to think of risk assessment as a stack of Swiss cheese slices. The holes in the cheese are opportunities for failure, and each of the slices serve as "defensive layers" against potential problems. One mistake may allow a problem to pass through a hole in one layer (or cheese slice), but in the next layer the holes are in different spots, so the problem is blocked. The assumption is that every defensive layer (or cheese slice) has holes in it, but ideally you stack the cheese slices so the holes don't go all the way through.

"When accidents happen, you have the act itself, like getting lost or breaking your leg. But then, what were the circumstances that set the stage for that act? Fatigue? Poor planning? You didn't fully appreciate the risks involved? It's never just one thing," Michael says.

When an accident occurs—a hiker gets lost or breaks a leg—certain contributing factors may happen instantaneously, while others may have developed slowly over time. A rock might tumble down the hill and break the bones in your ankle. That's a sudden, spur-of-the-moment hole in your Swiss cheese. But other contributing factors may have lain dormant for weeks, months, or even years, until they finally caused a problem. For example, if you've spent years hiking solo without carrying any emergency gear but never had a need for it, your experience has likely contributed to a false sense of security. That's a contributing factor that developed slowly and almost imperceptibly. But now—after an accident—you have a broken ankle and you're lacking emergency gear—two holes in your Swiss cheese.

"There are things we can control," Michael says, "and there are things we can't control, but we can plan for."

So, if you told your spouse that you were hiking to Blue Lake via the North Side Trail and that you'd be back by 6 p.m., you have a defensive layer in your Swiss cheese—or at least a way to mitigate the damage. You're stuck in the woods with a broken ankle, but it's only a matter of time until searchers rescue you. Because you told your spouse where you were going and when you'd be back, people will be looking for you a lot sooner than if you hadn't.

The Swiss Cheese Model makes the case that you should always have a Plan B. But too often, Michael notes, hikers go out for a walk in the park and don't think they need a Plan B. After all, it's only a walk in the park.

Day-hikers in particular tend to be the most unprepared. Michael points to the 2014 search for Magdalena Glinkowski, a thirty-three-year-old woman who went out for a hike in Mount Tamalpais State Park, a woodsy playground that lies a few miles north of San Francisco's Golden Gate Bridge.

"Glinkowski worked alone and lived alone, so no one knew that she'd gone out for a hike on that day," he recalls. "Five days later, park rangers notice that a car has been left at a trailhead parking lot for several days." The rangers investigated and found out that the car was registered to Glinkowski. After talking to her landlord, they discovered she hadn't been home for several days.

Michael explains the anatomy of how a search mission unfolds. "The first thing we do is establish a PLS, or point last seen. Or sometimes we use the 'place last known'—like a trailhead where the lost person has left their car. Once we have that, the search starts with a hasty search, where we check established trails and roads in the immediate area near the PLS. Probably 90 percent of searches get resolved with the initial hasty search. Then we try to track the missing person's cell phone, and we interview their friends and family."

Searchers create a "lost person profile" by contacting family members, friends, and coworkers to find out any relevant information about the missing person. This might include physical details like what clothes he or she was wearing, or psychological details like the person's state of mind.

In Glinkowski's case, searchers learned that she had recently lost her job and had trouble getting along with some coworkers. Michael and his search team had to consider the possibility that Glinkowski was despondent and had committed suicide. After all, overdue hikers are not uncommon at Mount Tamalpais, but five days was beyond the usual realm of overdue.

But soon, a critical piece of information arrived—park rangers had a surveillance camera pointed at the coin box where visitors pay their parking and camping fees. "We looked at the footage and we were able to get an image of her paying for her parking fee. We were thinking that perhaps she had killed herself, but somebody who goes to the trouble to pay their parking fee doesn't match that profile."

In Glinkowski's car, searchers also found a grocery store receipt from earlier in the day, which showed that she had bought food for her hike an hour before she parked.

"We knew that she had already been missing for five days. We had just over 100 searchers plus ten canine teams on our first day," he says. "We searched all the trails and major drainages where we thought she might be. A witness said that he saw Glinkowski in the area of Stinson Beach, about five miles from her car, so searchers spent a lot of time combing that area."

Two days of fruitless searching passed by. On the third day, the team took a break to regroup and plan a new strategy. That afternoon, another clue came in. "A trail runner said that that he had seen Glinkowski on a 'social' trail near Pantoll Ridge, just east of the park campground and not far from where her car was parked."

(A social trail is a path made by frequent human use. It's not a designated park trail and wouldn't appear on a park map, but hikers might easily assume it's a legitimate trail.)

As the days passed with no signs of Glinkowski, one of the detectives working the case re-interviewed the runner who said he saw the missing woman on a social trail. In this second interview, the runner said the trail wasn't a social trail, it was actually a deer trail.

When Michael heard this revised information, a lightbulb turned on. "What I realized at that moment was that she was totally confused and off-trail," he says.

Deer trails, or game trails, are paths made by animals. Coyotes, deer, and other four-footed creatures regularly travel the same routes in search of food or water. They are generally narrower and often much steeper than either social trails or park-designated trails. A hiker who follows a deer trail will likely find herself in dense, brushy terrain that will soon become impassible. Two feet can't go everywhere four feet can go.

Michael assembled all the clues and decided Glinkowski had to be up on Pantoll Ridge. "I knew she was there and that we just missed her. Even the dogs must have missed her," he says. "We went back with 160 people. We assigned fifty people just to that ridge, and within an hour and a half we found her."

Two cadaver dogs—dogs that are trained to detect human remains—alerted searchers to the spot. Glinkowski's body was found in terrain that Michael calls "brush under canopy." This colloquial term refers to a forested area that is so dense that no one could have spotted her.

"It was very steep terrain filled with brush. She was in a drainage only forty feet away from an established trail, but she couldn't be seen from that trail," he says.

Glinkowski's cause of death was hypothermia. It's possible that she wound up on that deer trail after becoming disoriented from diabetic issues, including low blood sugar.

"She could have walked downhill for 200 yards and hit a trail or walked uphill and hit the park campground in 150 yards. I think she was disoriented and not making good decisions," he says.

Michael says that most lost hikers are found within a few miles of their cars (Glinkowski's afternoon day-hike ended with her dying only about one mile from her car), but it's more complicated than that. "There are different categories of lost hikers. There are mushroom pickers, photographers, hunters, people with dementia, adventurers like mountaineers and rock climbers, and then just regular day-hikers. They tend to get lost in different ways."

Search-and-rescue teams use statistical probabilities from a lost-person-behavior database to develop an educated guess of where the missing person might be found. Michael says that the information is available at a searcher's fingertips via a free app called "Lost Person Behavior." According to the app, 50 percent of "regular hikers" are found within 1.9 miles of their Point Last Seen, which is often the trailhead where their car is parked, and 75 percent are found within 3.6 miles.

If we apply the Swiss Cheese Model to Glinkowski's tragic death, we see a lot of holes in her simple plan to hike in the state park for a couple of hours. She didn't tell anyone she was going for a hike, let alone where she was going and when she'd be back. She had a pre-existing diabetic condition that made it more likely for her to become disoriented. It seems she wasn't familiar enough with the park's terrain to be able to distinguish between maintained hiking trails and deer trails.

Michael says what happened to Glinkowski was preventable. Even casual day-hikers should think about the Swiss Cheese Model.

He says the questions to ask yourself are: *Have I evaluated the risks involved, and do I have ways to mitigate for those risks?* And maybe more importantly, *Do I really know what risks are involved?*

"If you're heading outside for a hike or a bike ride or whatever, figure out what the possible failures are. What are the possible hazards? Make sure you have a contingency plan if there's a failure. Run through possible scenarios before you leave. It doesn't take very long to think it through."

Risk Assessment

Bob Gehlen has a steady day job managing financial portfolios from a swanky office in a San Francisco high-rise. But when he needs to cancel a meeting, his clients understand. They know he's not playing golf; he's searching for someone who's gone missing.

When Bob started volunteering for Marin County Search and Rescue (SAR) five years ago, he was already a remarkable outdoor athlete—an accomplished runner, cyclist, climber, surfer, and skier. After completing his first weekend of SAR training, the fifty-four-year-old financial planner knew he had found his calling.

Volunteers prepare to evacuate an injured hiker by helicopter.

"What's the definition of a life well lived? I think I got lucky and found it," he says.

The Marin County SAR Team is one of only twenty specially certified Mountain Rescue teams in California, so its services are required all over the state, and especially in the high mountains of the Sierra Nevada. Mountain Rescue volunteers have specialized skills—they're rock climbers, skiers, or mountaineers who are trained to be self-sufficient for several days in the backcountry. Their job duties might include rescuing an injured hiker from a mountaintop or searching for evidence from a plane crash. It's the kind of work that fuels Bob's passion for search-and-rescue.

Bob's most memorable Mountain Rescue mission was the focus of a high-profile media story in the summer of 2015. He still gets emotional when he talks about it.

"I can't describe what it's like to be a significant part of someone else's rescue. It touches that piece of us that is so hard to get to," he says.

In August 2015, Miyuki Harwood went on a Sierra Club–sponsored backpacking trip in central California. The group headed up to Blackcap Basin, north of Kings Canyon National Park, and camped on the shore of Horsehead Lake at 10,400 feet.

"Miyuki was a sixty-two-year-old triathlete, in great shape, very bright and very competitive. It wasn't like she wanted to just finish the race at age sixty-two, she wanted to win," Bob says.

On the sixth day of the group's trip, they decided to take a day-hike to the top of Blackcap Mountain. On the way to the top, super-fit Miyuki got ahead of the other hikers.

"After she summited the peak, she rejoined the group and told the leader she was going to head back down on her own. She planned to meet everyone back at camp at 5:30, but she never showed up," Bob says. "The Sierra Club trip leader had a satellite phone, so he called in and reported her missing that night."

The Fresno sheriff's office couldn't send in helicopters immediately due to heavy smoke from a major wildfire burning nearby in Kings Canyon. But they sent in a team of field searchers who hiked twenty miles to reach Miyuki's group at Horsehead Lake.

"The search went on for eight days, and they found nothing. On some days the smoke cleared a bit, and they were able to bring in the helicopters. They had dogs searching the area as well as several Mountain Rescue teams. But there were no clues. The National Guard even had its drone fly over at 25,000 feet looking for a heat signature. Still nothing," Bob says.

Almost 97 percent of all lost hikers are found within the first twenty-four hours. If a hiker is missing for eight days, the prognosis usually isn't good. By that time the hiker is usually dead, or he or she is going to be extremely difficult to find.

As the days passed in the search for Miyuki, exhausted search-and-rescue volunteers were replaced with fresh volunteers, often from far-away counties. Bob's team was called in from Marin County, more than 200 miles away. They were dropped off by helicopter at Horsehead Lake on the afternoon of the eighth day.

Bob was leading about a dozen searchers, including a few youth members of the Marin SAR team. "It was already pretty late in the afternoon, so we hiked up on a ridgeline northwest of the lake to look at the drainage that was going to be our search area," he says.

Search areas are broken into segments related to the terrain. For example, a ridge or a watershed might separate one segment from another. Searchers always cover the easy-access routes, like trails and fire roads, first. Then they scour the harder-to-reach places, like a creek drainage farther away from the trail. They know that hikers typically follow the course of least resistance. Hikers are influenced by gravity and will usually head downhill.

"We looked down into the drainage and realized it was huge, so we strategized. There was an incredible amount of terrain. We decided to cover the southern portion first," he says.

The next morning, Bob positioned searchers up and down the ridgeline heading toward the drainage. Searchers bellowed Miyuki's name, hoping to get a response. "We were doing voice calls non-stop," Bob says. "About forty-five minutes into the search, one of our youth members called me on the radio and said, 'I think I heard a whistle.'"

"We did another voice call, and we heard another whistle. This time it was very clear. I told one of my searchers, who has a very deep voice, to call again and ask if this was Miyuki. A voice called back 'yes.' "

Bob felt his adrenaline kick in. "I thought, 'I can't believe this is happening.' I called into the command post on the radio and told them we had contacted Miyuki, and she was alive. Then I took a deep breath," he says. "I called the team and said, 'Okay, we all want to jump off this mountain and go get to her. But that's not what we're going to do. She's been here for eight days; she's going to survive another ten minutes. We're going to take our time and be safe.' "

When rescuers reached Miyuki, she had a broken ankle on one leg and a broken femur on the other. She also had a herniated disk. She had remained conscious and fought for her survival for eight days, but now that help had arrived, her body went into shock. The medics treated her and kept her comfortable until the helicopter arrived.

"She said to us that just that morning she had given up hope. She was ready to die," Bob says. "We loaded her into a litter, and a short while later she was on her way to the hospital."

More than a week prior, when Miyuki left her group and descended Blackcap Mountain, she somehow missed the turnoff for Horsehead Lake and wound up near the mountain's base in a massive boulder field. She fell off a large boulder and broke her ankle and leg. Unable to move, she stayed in that spot for the night, hoping that perhaps by morning she would be able to get up and walk. The only gear she carried was a day-pack with a water bottle, a filter, a whistle, and a jacket.

The nighttime temperature dropped into the high fifties. Miyuki was cold but able to bear it; the jacket in her day-pack was just enough to prevent hypothermia. But the next day she still couldn't move. She could hear the sound of water running somewhere in the distance, and she knew she needed to get water to survive. For the next two days, she crawled on her belly until she got to a creek.

"And that's where she stayed for the next six days," Bob says. "The creek bank wasn't comfortable, so she would spend the day about fifty feet away, near a large boulder. Every morning she would crawl down to the creek, filter a liter of water, then come back to this big rock and hang out. She'd lie in the sun to get warm because the nights were pretty cold."

After her helicopter flight to the hospital, Miyuki's troubles didn't end. Her injuries were severe enough that she had to undergo several rounds of surgery.

Bob grapples with the question of what Miyuki should have done differently. Even though he thinks there's a lot of merit to spending time alone in nature, he wonders whether hiking alone in the backcountry is ever a good idea, even for someone with Miyuki's tip-top physical conditioning.

"If she hadn't been alone, this never would have happened. She still may have gotten hurt, but she wouldn't have been out there for nine days," he says.

When you hike or climb or ski solo, the consequences of failure are much higher than when you are with a companion or two. If you're outdoors alone and you hurt yourself, you're in a vulnerable position. If you're off-trail, hurt, and alone, like Miyuki was, the vulnerability factor goes way up.

Bob notes that we can apply the Swiss Cheese Model of Accident Correlation to Miyuki's situation. Her plan certainly had a few holes in it—hiking alone, heading off-trail in unfamiliar terrain, not carrying adequate emergency supplies, having no means to summon help if she was injured—and, sadly, those holes lined up.

"A lot of people aren't knowledgeable enough about what could go wrong. They just assume that everything's going to go fine—maybe because it has always gone fine in the past," Bob says.

It's not just hiking alone that caused the catastrophe. But that was one risk factor, and when it met with the other holes in her stack of Swiss cheese slices, Miyuki experienced a perfect storm.

"The truth is that if you take risks, but there are no consequences, you will take the same risks over and over again until that risk ends up being catastrophic," Bob says. "The actual failure doesn't happen when it looks like it happened. It happened a long time before that. The law of probability finally catches up. Statistics finally play out."

Miyuki made mistakes, but she also did a lot of things right. She was carrying a few lifesaving tools—most notably her jacket and whistle. She was able to filter the stream water before she drank it because she was carrying a filter. The one piece of equipment that could have saved her several days of agony was some means of summoning help, like a personal locator beacon (see pages 20–22). Still, she used what she had to her best advantage—including a tremendous amount of personal fortitude.

Bob encourages hikers, especially solo hikers, to ask themselves these questions: Even though I might be beating the odds, what are the risks I'm taking? What are the risks that I'm not even noticing? What are the consequences that haven't yet happened?

"It all comes down to risk assessment," Bob says. "I use it for everything in my life. I have to look at what the risks are, even the ones I don't want to look at. I try to examine every aspect of my life and answer those questions," he says.

Dogs to the Rescue

Lisa Whatford has a few words of advice for hikers who might someday need to be rescued.

"Leave a dirty sock and a photo in a Ziploc bag in your car," she says.

Your photo tells Lisa what you look like. Your odiferous sock tells Lisa's dog what you smell like. The 200 million olfactory receptors in her furry German shepherd nose will lead her to the drainage where you wandered in circles, the box canyon where you backtracked, and the creek where you sat down and wondered how you got into this predicament.

"Dogs can smell what we can't see," Lisa says. "You're emitting odors, and your odors go out into the air. A dog's nose can smell you from possibly a quarter-mile away."

Lisa's shepherd Beaujet is particularly skilled at distinguishing odors, but even the average mutt can distinguish every human from every other human by microscopic quantities of our unique odor

Beaujet and her canine friends prepare for a search-and-rescue operation.

"fingerprints." From a dog's perspective, no one else smells exactly like you.

"Beaujet can smell at concentrations of one part per trillion," Lisa says. "If you're in the wilderness and you stay put, my dog's going to find you. If you wander around, we might miss each other because Beaujet will take me to where you were, and now you're not there anymore. It makes it a lot harder."

Dogs are able to "sense" the skin cells we slough off. Humans constantly lose rafts of dead skin cells—about 50 million every minute. Many of these microscopic flakes settle to the ground. Smaller and lighter rafts are carried away in the wind, and a dog's keen nose can detect these rafts. Additionally, when humans walk, we make footprints. As each foot gets set down, soil is moved, or vegetation is crushed. To a dog, that footprint smells different from the ground around it.

Every dog owner knows that a dog can detect a squirrel perched high up in a tree long before its owner would ever notice it. "Dogs are much more in tune with their surroundings. They're more aware of sudden changes in the environment than humans are," Lisa says. "I could walk right by you and not notice you. Dogs detect movement. You move a little bit and they're going to pick up on it."

When Lisa and Beaujet are working a search, their "finds" are often nonresponsive people. "The foot searchers find lost people who can holler back to be found. It's the people who are nonresponsive, who are injured or had a stroke or something that we wind up finding with the dogs," she says.

Lisa, a search-and-rescue (SAR) leader who lives in the mountains near Lake Tahoe and works with three different California SAR teams, has been looking for lost and missing people for more than two decades. She got interested in search-and-rescue after she adopted a retired, six-year-old search dog.

"His handler moved to Hawaii, and I adopted him," she says. "Two months later, a handicapped boy, Kenny Miller, went missing in my area. It snowed the night he went missing. I was so frustrated that I had a search dog and did not know how to use him during the two-week-long search effort. Kenny died on that first night. It was a tragedy."

That sad event provided the impetus for Lisa to start search-and-rescue training, both for herself and her dog. Beaujet is her third rescue dog, and Lisa trains her every day, often in tandem with fellow SAR worker Chris Kozlowski and her dog Mika.

Mika, a blonde-furred shepherd, trained for three years before starting SAR work. "Mika's more relaxed now that she's five, but the first three years were rough," Chris says. Once when Chris left Mika in the car, the shepherd got bored and tore apart the car's interior, causing several thousand dollars' worth of damage. "She even chewed up the gear shift," Chris says. "These dogs are very willful and they're smart. They're good problem-solvers. They need work to do."

The dogs' training might seem like fun to them, but it is serious business for Lisa and Chris. "Today we're going to do area work,"

Lisa Whatford with Beaujet (left) and Chris Kozlowski with Mika (right).

Lisa says. "We'll probably hide for each other. I'll hide and Mika will find me. And Chris will hide and Beaujet will find her. We go find a forested area, we use our radios, and we hide from the dogs. If we can, we use volunteers. It's good for the dogs to find strangers."

Beaujet and Mika are trained in three disciplines: avalanche, forensics, and wilderness. Dogs trained in avalanche can find people "under the surface," Lisa says. Dogs trained in wilderness can find people on the ground, and dogs trained in forensics can find human remains and evidence.

To train the dogs for cadaver work, the women hide bones, also called "cadaver training aids," in the forest. The dogs find them. But they find plenty of other human evidence, too. Every day when

16

I go out for a run at the ski resort, my dog finds stuff. She'll find a headband, a cell phone, cameras, a shirt, chewing gum, Kleenex. The dogs are trained to find what isn't natural in the forest, which is us and what we leave behind," she says.

Hardworking search-and-rescue dogs take a break to pose for photographs.

"Beaujet is hard-wired to work, which is good. If I go out for a run, she puts herself to work. I don't tell her to work. She knows to let me know if there's something unusual going on in her world."

Search-and-rescue work, for both the dogs and the two women, is on a strictly volunteer basis. To pay the bills, Lisa works as a hair stylist. Chris is a physical therapist. Their dogs need special search-and-rescue gear, like vests and goggles, as well as training and certifications, which the women pay for out of their own funds.

"Working search-and-rescue is a lot of commitment—time and money. It's volunteer. We don't get paid," Chris says.

When Lisa, Chris, and their dogs find lost people in the wilderness, those people are usually extremely grateful to be found. But occasionally there's the idiot factor, also known as the Dunning-Kruger Effect: a cognitive bias in which people don't or won't admit to their own ineptitude.

"On one search, the guy was all tweaked when we found him. He kept saying, 'I can't believe I'm being rescued by a woman.' And I was thinking, 'Yeah. I can't believe I'm out here at 3 a.m. rescuing you.' I had to spend three hours walking that man out of the wilderness while he questioned whether or not my dog is a pure-bred," Chris says.

Still, both women agree that their rewards come in finding people, whether or not they show gratitude, and sometimes even whether they are alive or not.

"We bring people home. We unite families, or we give them closure," Lisa says. "Not a lot of people can do what we do, or even want to do what we do. It's a nice way to give back."

The Rescuer Needs a Rescue

John Platt is one of the most self-reliant guys you'll ever meet. He's a MacGyver-type who can figure stuff out—how to fix a broken camp stove, how to find the best route across a scree-covered slope, how to stay warm while camping in the snow. He's even skilled at cooking gourmet camp dinners (check out his recipes on pages 146–7 in the Water and Food chapter).

"I like to hike and climb by myself. I'm kind of a Luddite and I don't bring a cell phone or a radio," he says. "I don't want to be one of those people who takes extra risks because they think, 'Hey, I have a cell phone, I can call for a rescue.' I like to be self-sufficient."

John is an avid climber, skier, cyclist, and backpacker, and volunteers for his local search-and-rescue team in Valley County, Idaho. He says the reason that most people need rescues from the wilderness is because "a series of things have gone wrong. The rule of thumb is that it's not one thing that goes wrong, but a chain of things that go wrong."

And even the most experienced adventurers can have stuff go wrong. Missteps happen. John knows that firsthand.

On a day trip, John and a buddy were hiking the approach to a rock-climbing site. They had been on the trail for only about forty-five minutes.

"We were walking up a dry streambed, and I stepped onto a log that had a little skim of ice on it. My foot slid sideways and my toe got caught. My heel kept moving out but my toe didn't, so I had this huge torsional force on my leg. I pitched over backwards," he recalls. "My friend was behind me, and he heard my bone break."

It was just a simple little step, the same kind of step he'd taken a thousand times before—not a risky maneuver. "I never thought, *Wow, this step might be dangerous.*"

The two men had to get back to their car, and that meant heading back down the rugged, rock-strewn streambed. "It wasn't a trail, so it was hard going. I tried to crawl for a while, but I made it about 200 yards in half an hour. I couldn't crawl on my knees in all that rubble, so I tried scooting along on my butt. It was really slow," he remembers. "Finally my buddy supported me on one side, and I held a big stick on the other side. I basically hopped out with his help."

When the two men reached their car, John phoned a doctor friend, who told him to pack his ankle in ice and get home to Boise.

John eventually had surgery, and wasn't able to put weight on his ankle for three months. When he looks back on the accident, John realizes that not being alone when he hurt himself was the key to his relatively quick rescue.

"If I'd been by myself, it would have been really serious. I didn't have my cell phone with me, but even if I did, there's no cell reception out there. It would have taken me eight or ten hours to get back to the truck. I probably would have had to spend to the night outside," he says.

"It's a good lesson for me and everybody else. This is why if you're hiking alone, you need to have enough stuff with you so that you can be decently comfortable for a night or two. Being safe is really about what equipment you have, and whether or not you've told people where you are going."

How to Get Found

When John Platt reflects back on the search-and-rescue missions he's been a part of, he says, "We've had a lot of rescues where people went somewhere else than where they said they were going to go. When we're working search-and-rescue, we're constantly getting bad information. But since it's the only information we have, we have to use it."

John says that if you want to get rescued, you need to go where you told people you would go, and you need to be visible.

"If you want to be found, don't wear green or brown or gray clothing. We can't see hikers dressed like that even when we're right on top of them. If you're not going to wear bright colors, at least take bright colors with you."

And even though he doesn't carry one, he thinks cell phones can save your life, too—as long as you can get service where you need it.

"If you have a medical emergency when you're by yourself, you're done, most likely," he says. "Carrying a cell phone with you is a valid thing to do. If you call 911, you don't even have to say anything. They can track you. Someone will know where you are."

Personal Locator Beacons & Satellite Messengers

Yes, your cell phone might save you in an emergency. But then again, it might leave a big hole in your Swiss cheese. What if there's no cell service in the rocky ravine where you break your ankle?

John Platt says that even though cell coverage across the United States gets better every year, even in remote mountain regions, there are still plenty of places where cell phones don't work. For those places, hikers need a personal locator beacon, or PLB: "If you're by yourself, having a PLB is a great way to get rescued."

Personal locator beacons and satellite messengers are small and lightweight, and they can save lives.

Like GPS devices, PLBs are technological marvels that rely on satellites to do their jobs, not cell towers. As long as they have a clear shot at the sky, they can send out an SOS signal and/or let your friends and family know you're okay.

If you need to be rescued, you simply activate your PLB, which you registered when you bought the device, and it transmits your unique identification code along with your GPS coordinates to the Air Force Rescue Coordination Center. The Center then dispatches the call to the closest rescue center, which is often the local sheriff's department. Then the local search-and-rescue team goes out and finds you.

The latest emphasis in PLB technology is making them do more than just pinpoint a lost or injured hiker's location. This upgrades them to the product category known as satellite messengers (or SENDs for "satellite emergency notification devices"), a step up from a basic PLB. For example, the new Spot Gen3 gives its owner a choice of five signal messages that he or she can send.

"The old ones gave you only 'I'm okay' or 'Send a rescue,' but there's a lot of gray area in between those two when you're out in the mountains," John says. "The new ones can actually let you provide information, like 'I'm having trouble but I'm going to be fine. I'm just going to be late.'"

The most expensive versions of satellite messengers allow for two-way communication. The DeLorme inReach Explorer lets you send and receive short text messages by satellite, so you can stay in touch with family and friends whether or not it's an emergency. It's great for calling for help, but it's also great for saying "I love you" or "I'll be home on Thursday."

Michael St. John of Marin County SAR is a fan of the DeLorme inReach. "The technology is amazing. Your loved ones can follow you on the Pacific Crest Trail, where cell phones don't work, and observe your progress. You can even text back and forth if you want."

With devices like the Spot Gen3 and the DeLorme inReach, you must purchase a subscription to active your service, making them more expensive. With a basic PLB, you don't need a subscription, but you still must register your device with the National Oceanic and Atmospheric Administration (NOAA) after you purchase it. Registration costs nothing. The NOAA links your device's identification number with your personal information, like your name and address and any medical condition you have may have. If your PLB gets activated, the government knows that it's yours. Statistics show that more than 70 percent of PLBs aren't registered, which renders them useless.

For search-and-rescue professionals, the two-way communication of satellite messengers means that they can know in advance whether a hiker is just lost, or lost and injured, or injured and in need of some very specialized medical equipment as soon as possible. "Every rescue is different," Michael says. "If people can tell us what they need, that can save a lot of time."

"Some people would question the use of these devices. They say they're out in nature to be disconnected. I agree that it's necessary to take breaks from our current society where we are always on and connected. But when you're in trouble, a PLB is a really good thing," Michael says.

Some outdoorspeople have abused the power of their PLBs and satellite messengers, earning the devices the nickname "yuppie 911." They are meant to be used only in very serious emergencies, when life or limb is threatened and all other means of self-rescue have been exhausted. In other words, the PLB is supposed to be your last resort. And yet, people have activated their PLBs because they were "running low" on water or because they were concerned about bears.

Personal locator beacons have acquired so many fans that the state of Oregon tried to pass a law that would require hikers, climbers, and skiers to carry them when climbing or skiing above 10,000 feet in the winter months. The bill was instigated due to the huge number of search-and-rescue operations on Oregon's Mount Hood. While many search-and-rescue teams were in favor of the bill, others opposed it because they feared that mandatory use of PLBs would give inexperienced climbers a false sense of security and inspire them to take more risks—and thus create the need for more rescues.

"It's not smart to rely on technology to save you," John says. "It's not 100 percent reliable. You can drop it and break it. Your batteries can run out. Don't use it as an excuse to overextend yourself, to do more than you would do otherwise, go farther than you said you would, take a bigger risk. But if you're by yourself and in real trouble, these devices can save you."

Solo Hiking: Tell Someone Where and When

A lot of people will tell you that you should never hike alone. And that conventional wisdom makes perfect sense, especially for inexperienced hikers. If you have a serious injury—or even if you just twist an ankle—your hiking partner can hike out and get rescue help. Having a partner is also beneficial because two people usually make better decisions than one. With another person at your side, you may choose a better route than you would by yourself. And if you get lost, two heads are probably smarter than one for figuring out how to stay warm and dry until you get found.

But the more we interviewed highly experienced outdoors experts, the more we heard that while they don't recommend solo hiking, they frequently do it themselves. It might seem like they were breaking their own rules, but they did so by following a critical, unbreakable caveat:

If you're going to hike anywhere alone, make sure you tell someone exactly where you are going and when you expect to be back. Lisa Whatford, a search-and-rescue expert who hikes almost every day, frequently alone, has a simple system: When she leaves the trailhead, she texts her husband or friend a simple message stating her route and her destination, something along the lines of: "On my way to West Lake via Green Creek Trail. Be back by 4 p.m." Then, when she finishes her hike, she texts again: "Back home. Thanks." Her husband or friend doesn't even need to respond.

It's a great system, and it can save a solo hiker's life. Even hikers who choose to carry a personal locator beacon should have this friend-alert system in place. (For minor emergencies, you might

Solo hiking offers many personal rewards, but it requires taking extra precautions.

prefer to have your friend come get you instead of alerting the federal government.)

But for the system to work properly, protocols must be followed. First, the solo hiker has to go exactly where she said she would go, and follow the exact trail she said she would take. Many a search-and-rescue operation has been stalled or made a lot more complicated because a hiker told his family he was going to Blue Lake, but when he got there, he changed his mind and went to Green Lake. It's easy to get caught up in the moment when you're hiking and decide to push farther or explore new territory, but you might wind up hampering the efforts of searchers who are trying to find you.

The second critical protocol is that the person who knows where you're hiking must be diligent about making sure you've arrived home. If you say you'll be back at your house at 4 p.m., that person should be looking for your "I'm home" text by 4 p.m., and/or calling you to say, "Hey, where the heck are you? Are you back?" The person you're trusting with your text message can't be someone who won't check their phone for a couple of days, or someone who will just assume you're okay. If you don't check in, that person needs to act.

A disproportionately large amount of search-and-rescue operations don't get started until it's too late—and that's often because the person who is lost or injured has not told anyone where he is going and when he will be back. And if you happen to live alone or with a roommate who doesn't pay much attention to your whereabouts, it might take a few days before anyone realizes you're not around.

If you have the knowledge and experience to want to hike solo, that's fine. A solo hike is not automatically dangerous, especially for experienced hikers. But an experienced hiker should know enough to carry a pack with everything he needs to self-rescue or at least keep himself alive through an unplanned overnight. He probably should carry a personal locator beacon. And he definitely should notify a reliable hiking friend about where he is going and what time he will be back.

2
Wilderness Smarts

The Day-Hiker's Checklist

Aside from the shoes on your feet, it doesn't take much equipment to go day hiking. While backpackers must concern themselves with tents, sleeping pads, cooking gear, and more, day-hikers have an easier time of it. Still, too many people set out for a day on the trail carrying too little equipment. As any search-and-rescue team member will tell you, the vast majority of SAR missions involve day-hikers, not backpackers.

"There's something about day-hiking that makes people feel like they don't need to prepare," says search-and-rescue expert Lisa Whatford. "They think they're just going out for a few hours, and it's daytime, so there's nothing to think about."

Even the simplest of day hikes can turn into a tragedy with a badly sprained ankle, a fall, or a major change in the weather. What would be a minor accident in the suburbs can become a catastrophe in the backcountry. If their hike doesn't go according to plan, day-hikers need to be ready with a pack full of essentials that can save their bacon.

Even on short day hikes, carry everything you might need for an unplanned overnight.

The key question to ask yourself is: *Do I have enough stuff in my pack so that I'll be okay if I spend the night outside?* If you carry everything on the list below, then the answer is *yes*.

1. **Food and water**. Carry of a couple of full water bottles plus a purifier or filtering device to obtain water from streams, rivers, or lakes. (See Chapter 5: Water and Food, for many easy options for purifying water.) For food, take whatever you like. Some people go gourmet and carry the complete inventory of a fancy grocery store. Others stick with high-energy snacks like nutrition bars, nuts, dried fruit, turkey or beef jerky, and crackers. The best rule is to bring more than you think you can eat. You can always carry it out with you or give it to somebody on the trail who needs it.
2. **A good trail map**. Never rely on trail signs or even an ultra-fancy GPS device to get you where you want to go. If you ever find yourself lost, a map is your best chance at self-rescue.

3. **Extra clothing for layering**. Weather conditions can change at any time. Not only can the weather suddenly turn windy, cloudy, or rainy, but your own body conditions also change: you'll perspire as you hike up a sunny hill, then get chilled at the top of a windy ridge or when you descend into shade. Wear or carry clothing made from high-tech fabrics that wick moisture away from your skin, and always carry a warm outer-layer jacket, preferably one that is waterproof and wind resistant.

4. **Gloves, hat, and rain gear**. Gloves and a hat are non-negotiable; they can make a cold night a lot less cold. If you don't want to carry rain gear, at least pack along one of the $3, single-use emergency rain ponchos that come in a package the size of a deck of cards.

5. **Flashlight or headlamp**. Always carry a couple of these, just in case your hike takes longer than you planned. Headlamps are great because they leave your hands free. Mini-flashlights weigh almost nothing and can save the day. Tiny "squeeze" LED flashlights, which are about the size and shape of a quarter, clip onto any key ring. (The Photon Micro-Light is a popular brand.) Whatever kind of flashlight you carry, make sure the batteries work before you set out on the trail. Take along an extra set of batteries and an extra bulb, or simply an extra flashlight or two.

6. **Sunglasses, sunscreen, sun hat, and lip balm**. Of course you know the dangers of the sun, and the higher the elevation, the more dangerous it is. Wear sunglasses to protect your eyes and sunscreen with a high SPF on any exposed skin. Put on your sunscreen thirty minutes before you go outdoors so it has time to take effect. Skin-savvy hikers also protect their faces with a lightweight, wide-brimmed hat. Don't forget to protect your lips, too, by wearing a lip balm with a high SPF.

7. **First-aid kit**. Nothing major is required here unless you're fully trained in first aid, but a few supplies for blister repairs (moleskin or Spenco 2nd Skin), an elastic bandage, an antibiotic ointment, and an anti-inflammatory medicine such as ibuprofen can be valuable tools in minor and major emergencies. If anyone in

your party is allergic to bee stings or anything else in the outdoors, carry his or her medication.

8. **Swiss Army–style pocketknife**. Carry one with several blades, a can opener, scissors, and tweezers.

9. **Compass**. Know how to use it. If you don't know how, take a class or get someone to show you.

10. **Emergency supplies**. Ask yourself, *What would I need if I had to spend the night outside?* Aside from food, water, and other items previously listed, here are some basic emergency supplies that will get you through an unplanned night in the wilderness:

   • A Mylar sleeping bag or tarp. "Space blankets" made of foil-like Mylar film are designed to reflect radiating body heat. These can also serve as an emergency shelter. The non-reflective side can be used to signal a helicopter.

   • A fire-starting kit. A couple of packs of matches, a lighter, a candle, and some cotton balls soaked in Vaseline. Keep these in a waterproof container or Ziploc bag, just in case you ever need to build a fire for warmth or for signaling. A knife with a long blade will help you cut branches for firewood (your Swiss Army knife won't do the job).

   • A whistle. If you ever need help, you can blow a whistle for a lot longer than you can shout. Voices don't carry well in wind or near a running stream. A whistle is a cheap investment that can save your life.

   • A personal locator beacon, or PLB. See our discussion in Chapter 1: Risk and Rescue, on how a PLB can be a lifesaver.

Hike More Efficiently: Trekking Poles

In discussing trekking poles (or hiking sticks, as some people call them), hikers tend to fall into two camps: First, those who wouldn't think of hiking without them; and second, those who think poles are needless accessories sold to gullible novices.

The truth is, trekking poles can increase your speed and efficiency when you hike. And furthermore, they can take a lot of the pain and

Used properly, trekking poles can improve your speed, balance, and efficiency on the trail.

discomfort away from injuries that might otherwise stop you from hiking. But that's only true if you use them correctly, and many hikers don't.

Ann Marie spent (or misspent) her early hiking life belittling the use of trekking poles. Her attitude was simply, why carry anything you don't need to carry? But in her thirties, she broke an ankle and the resulting surgery and recovery time keep her off the trail for a few months. When she could finally take a few steps without crutches, she started daydreaming about her first hike. Her orthopedic surgeon told her to pick a fairly level, smooth trail and use trekking poles. She followed his advice, and voilà—a love affair with poles was born. Trekking poles can make an injury a non-issue.

Shin splints? Twisted ankle? Sore feet? Bad knee? Trekking poles can help with all that and more by allowing your arms to do some of the work that your legs and feet would otherwise have to do. Studies at Virginia's James Madison University and the UK's Northumbria University have shown that using trekking poles can reduce the stress on your lower body by about 25 percent—even more when you're going downhill, somewhat less when you're going uphill.

For most hikers with injuries, trekking poles come in handiest on the downhills. The poles help with braking, so you don't have to expend as much energy trying not to pitch forward as you fight gravity. Instead of jamming your weight into your forefoot and the front of your knees, as is natural on steep descents, you plant your poles in front of you and they carry your weight.

On uphills, poles are all about sharing the load. If you're carrying a heavy pack up a steep grade, why not utilize four "legs" instead of two? Effectively, that's what poles are able to do. And whether you're heading up or down, trekking poles also help you maintain your balance, which can be especially important if you're weighed down by a heavy backpack.

Poles have plenty of other uses, too. When crossing a high or fast stream, you can plant your poles in the streambed and use them for stability and balance. When you're walking on loose or slippery ground (think sandy desert washes or lingering snow in the mountains), poles provide more traction. When your tent pole breaks, a trekking pole makes a fine substitute. (For hikers who carry tarps or shelters instead of tents, trekking poles aren't a substitute—they're brought along to pitch the shelter.) When you need to cross a stream, planting a trekking pole in the streambed for stability against the current can make the difference between a successful ford and an unexpected swim. And when you need to take a selfie, some trekking poles have a built-in camera mount under the handle, so the pole can be used as a monopod. How's that for multiple uses?

Your pole can even serve as a weapon to scare off bothersome rodents who are clamoring for your food. If you're sitting on a slab of granite noshing on a turkey-and-avocado sandwich and the chipmunks start begging too aggressively, just wave your poles around and say, "Hey, anybody want a chipmunk on a stick?" Works every time.

If you decide to carry poles—and we strongly recommend you do, especially for longer day hikes and overnight trips—make sure you get a pair that will work best for you. Ann Marie swears by poles that are collapsible or retractable, so that you can shorten them and tie them on to your pack when you don't need them. She finds that she is much more likely to bring them along if she can stash or stow them in her pack occasionally.

With trekking poles, size matters. Most poles adjust from about twenty-four inches long to fifty-five inches long. When you go uphill, you'll want to adjust them so they are shorter. When you go downhill, you'll want to make them longer. To figure out how long your poles should be on your ups, downs, and even level sections, check your elbows. When you plant your poles, your elbows should be at a 90-degree angle, with your forearm parallel to the ground. Some people believe their poles are more comfortable when they're even shorter on ascents, so give that a try and see how it feels. Poles that are too long are a definite no-no, but poles that are too short may work better for you on the ups. Start with a 90-degree angle and then experiment.

If you've just hiked uphill to Poop Out Pass and now you need to hike steeply down the other side to Chill Out Meadow, take a minute to adjust your poles for the descent—make them longer by a couple of inches. This will make a huge difference in how useful they are. Poles that are too short don't help on descents; they'll just disrupt your balance. By the same token, poles that are too long don't help on ascents; they'll just wear out your arms and shoulders.

Weight matters, too. Don't even consider buying poles that weigh any more than eighteen ounces per pair; your arms will grow tired of using them after only a few miles. Some ultralight poles weigh in at less than sixteen ounces per pair. Trekking poles are generally made of either aluminum or carbon fiber, with carbon being lighter by a couple of ounces and usually more expensive. Some hikers say that carbon fiber is less durable than aluminum and more likely to break, but if you plant your poles carefully and don't let them get jammed into crevices, carbon fiber should hold up quite well. Ann Marie has owned the same pair of aluminum poles for fifteen years, and they've hiked with her over thousands of miles.

Proper Trekking Pole Technique

Using trekking poles properly seems intuitive to some people, especially cross-country skiers who are accustomed to using their poles for extra oomph with every stride. For other people, using trekking poles is something of a mystery. If used wrong, the poles will quickly get tossed into the pack as another piece of useless equipment. You can always tell the people who are getting the optimal efficiency out of their poles—they're hiking way ahead of everybody else, moving very fast and with a graceful, rhythmic stride, each foot step working in perfect coordination with a pole plant. Here's the key: You plant the right pole as you move your left foot forward. And then you plant the left pole as you move your right foot forward. The poles work in opposition to your feet, making your core muscles engage. Now it's not just your legs that are doing the walking—it's your whole body.

Try to match every step with a pole plant, especially on uphills and level stretches. This isn't always possible, of course, because sometimes the trailside brush or vegetation can get in the way, or rocky terrain makes it impossible to plant your poles rhythmically. On downhills, it may be too awkward to keep a one-on-one rhythm, especially when the grade is very steep, so just use the poles as much as you can. Any time you're putting weight on your poles when you go downhill, you're taking a lot of stress off your joints.

Sleep Well in the Backcountry

You'd think that with all the exercise you get hiking around the backcountry, you'd sleep like a baby as soon as you crawl into your tent. But unfortunately, that's not always the case.

Campsite Selection

Getting a good night of backpacking sleep starts with smart campsite selection. Shade and water are two near-musts when camping in the summer. The shade keeps your tent and your food cooler; a nearby lake or stream makes it easier to filter water and cook your meals.

A bad night's sleep might lead to a midday nap on a boulder pile.

Now here's what you don't want in a campsite: You don't want to camp in a low spot that's going to collect water if it rains, or soon you'll be sleeping in a lake. Any time you set up your tent, ask yourself the critical question: if it rains, where will the water go? Sure, you want a flat spot, but it shouldn't be the lowest spot around. Not only does rainwater gravitate toward low spots, so does condensation and cold air. Remember: low spots often lead to being wet and cold.

On the other hand, you don't want to put your tent on the highest spot around either, or it can become a lightning rod in a thunderstorm. Also on the list of "never camp here" spots: dry washes. If you're sleeping in a dry wash when a storm occurs upstream, you won't be able to escape the flash flood. Always stay away from washes when you camp in the desert.

If you're in mosquito country, look around for ponds, puddles, wet meadows, or similar insect-breeding sites. You don't want to set your tent in the middle of a mosquito nursery. On buggy trips, find a tent site that is away from slow-moving or stagnant water and moist vegetation. Ideally, locate a site that gets a little bit of wind—that will keep the bugs away.

The wind factor can be tricky. You want enough wind to keep the mosquitoes at bay, but you don't want your tent so exposed that you're buffeted by wind all night long. If that happens, you won't sleep. In windy spots, you will probably be happier camping in the trees or in the shelter of a big boulder—someplace where your tent is protected from the howling gale.

And it may seem obvious, but if you're camping at the beach, you don't want to be close enough to the tide line that you get surprised by waves lapping at your tent flaps.

While we're talking about campsite selection, it's critically important to minimize your impact when you select a site. Every camper wants to be near water so it's easier to cook food and filter water. But set your tent at least 200 feet from any body of water (about fifty paces) to help protect the water quality.

We know it looks like it would be great to set your tent ten feet from the shore of Photogenic Lake, but don't. It's not good for the lake—almost all human activities are polluting in some way—and it's not good for other backpackers who may show up. (They'll see your tent in every one of their vacation photos.) Your goal is to stay out of sight of other backpackers, if possible, and also to allow wildlife easy passage to and from the water.

At most backpacking destinations, you'll be able to find established campsites that have been used over the years by previous backpackers. These are ideal places to camp because the ground has already been impacted, so you aren't doing additional damage. If you're in a pristine area where you can't find any previously used campsites, thank the heavens above for this wonderful gift—it's an increasing rarity in America's wilderness. Then pitch your tent on bare ground or smooth rock so that you don't leave a trace. A wilderness advocacy organization called Leave No Trace provides some great tips on how to minimize your impact in the backcountry. Check them out at www.lnt.org.

Set up your tent at least 200 feet (about fifty paces) from a lake, stream, or other water source.

Set Up Camp Early

When backpacking, always try to arrive at your camping destination a couple of hours before sunset, usually by 4 or 5 p.m. That way if your favorite spot is taken, you have plenty of time to find another spot. You'll also have ample time for cooking, eating, and storing your food away from critters before the sky is pitch black. Making dinner in the dark is not especially fun.

Preparing for Bed

Getting your body temperature just right for sleeping in the back-country is a delicate operation. Ann Marie is a fussy sleeper, so she has to have all her "sleep aids" on her body or within reach. She especially likes to wear clean clothes (usually long underwear) inside her sleeping bag. If it's cold, she's always tempted to wear her fleece top and puffy jacket, too, but knows this is counterproductive. Instead, she'll drape her puffy on top of her bag for an extra layer of insulation.

There's always extra air space in her bag—space that her body isn't filling—so she'll stuff her extra clothes in the space. This keeps her warmer at night, and it means she doesn't have to put on cold clothes in the morning. When temperatures drop below freezing, she'll put any of her gear that uses batteries (SteriPEN water filter, camera, personal locator beacon) inside her bag, too. She'll cover her head with a wool hat, or keep it right next to her head in case she needs it during the night. If it's really cold, she'll cinch her sleeping bag hood around her head.

Finally, and this is the most important step of all, she prepares for middle-of-the-night "restroom" trips. When Nature calls, and it always does when you're sleeping in a tent, you'll need your shoes. Keep your camp sandals right outside the tent door. And you will probably need your headlamp, too, so have that somewhere that's easy to access. We've heard plenty of stories of hikers who get out of their tents to pee in the middle of the night and then fall into a creek or stumble over a boulder. It's good to be able to see where you're going.

One more tip for sleeping well in the backcountry: Get a back-packing pillow. It's the best four ounces you'll ever carry on your back. See Chapter 4: Gear That Matters, for pillow buying advice.

Dealing with Human Waste

Yes, a bear does poop in the woods, and at some point during your trip, you will, too. And that's why you need to carry a six-inch trowel and perhaps a very small bit of toilet paper (unless you're one of those hikers who prefers the large, soft leaves of corn lilies for wiping your nether regions).

As you've probably guessed by now, we're going to leave all delicacy aside when discussing this important matter. Wrap your mind around this: On Mount Whitney, the tallest peak in the contiguous United States at 14,505 feet in elevation, every hiker is required by law to pack along a "human waste pack-out kit" so they can carry their poop back to the trailhead and deposit it in special dumpsters. In a typical summer, Mount Whitney hikers pack out more than 7,000 pounds of human waste. That is a prodigious amount of poop that is NOT lying around decorating the slopes of Mount Whitney. Thank heavens.

You don't have to carry a human waste pack-out kit in most of America's wilderness. All you have to do is use a six-inch trowel to dig a hole. Why six inches? Because if it's shallower than that, your poop can be dug up by animals who are attracted to the yummy scent of partially digested food particles in your feces (yuck).

Outdoor stores sell super-lightweight trowels that will do the job—and many of them fold up so they're easy to pack. Depending on the ground you're digging in, your work may be easy or it may be difficult. In many places in New England, the soil is hard and full of rocks and roots. In many places in the Sierra Nevada or Rocky Mountains, the soil is hard-packed granite. A cheap plastic trowel will cost you about five bucks at most outdoors stores, and it may last for years. But if you know you'll always be digging in rock-hard soil, you might want to spend bigger bucks (about $25) and buy a titanium trowel like the QiWiz Big Dig. This finely crafted tool will last so long that you can pass it on to your grandchildren (and what a fine legacy that will be). Bonus: It weighs only half an ounce, and you'll be the envy of backpackers everywhere.

The old-timers out there will say, "I don't need no stinkin' trowel. When I poop in the woods, I just turn over a rock and use the hole that it left in the ground." Yeah, yeah. That might have been good enough back when disco was big, but have you looked at the world's population numbers lately? The wilderness is hammered with people, and trails are hammered with poop—especially big-name trails like the Appalachian Trail, the Pacific Crest Trail, and the John Muir Trail.

Nobody wants to see poop sitting on the ground right where you want to set up your tent. Nobody wants the bacteria from poop leeching into a pristine stream where you get your drinking water.

Got your trowel? Good. You probably don't need a lot of instructions here, but here goes: select an out-of-the-way location, dig a hole, poop in it, and cover it up. That's about it. What makes a good location? It should be at least 200 feet from any water source

A plastic trowel weighs only a few ounces and makes it easy to bury human waste.

(creek, lake, etc.), trail, or camping area. That's about fifty paces, or a short and pleasant walk.

The only place your hole should be dug less than six inches deep is in the desert, where there is very little organic soil to help biodegrade your poop. In desert regions, your cathole should be only about four inches deep so the sun can help with decomposition.

One fine point that merits a discussion: toilet paper. If you must use it, use as little as possible. When you're done, it's best to set a match to it (unless it's extremely windy and you fear you will burn down the forest in the process). Toilet paper decomposes a lot slower than poop does. If you bury your toilet paper in your poop hole, you run the risk of having an animal dig it up, resulting in ugly toilet paper scraps all over the ground. To circumvent this problem, learn what plants make good toilet paper. There's a good reason the velvety soft leaves of woolly mullein are known as "cowboy toilet paper," and the heart-shaped leaves of large-leaf aster are known as "lumberjack

A few campsites in Sequoia National Park are equipped with backcountry toilets, but they are the exception, not the rule.

toilet paper." In the Sierra Nevada, some hikers prefer the silky leaves of the corn lily (*veratrum californicum*), but in a pinch, just about any large-leaved plant will do. Except poison oak or poison ivy, of course.

In a few places in America, land managers have gone to the trouble to provide backcountry outhouses. If you happen to be camped in Sequoia National Park, you might find a luxurious outhouse such as the one shown here. It's a bit drafty, but there's no hole-digging required.

Hiking Smart in High Altitude

No other mountain range compares to the Himalayas of Nepal, home to nine of the ten highest peaks on earth, including the highest of them all, 29,029-foot Mount Everest. Miles of trails climb from verdant Hindu foothills to remote Buddhist villages and glacial highlands. For backpackers, it is the mecca of all mountain ranges.

In 1999, thirty-five-year-old Kim Wyatt planned a month-long hiking trek in the Himalayas. A skilled backpacker, Kim grew up hiking with her father in the Sierra Nevada Mountains. At eighteen, she moved to Yosemite National Park, and, some years later, the Rocky Mountains and then Alaska. Kim had already hiked many of America's tallest peaks, and now she was ready for bigger adventures.

"For me, the next obvious thing was to go to Nepal," Kim explains.

Kim's friend Carlisle proposed the trip: a backpacking adventure on the Annapurna Circuit, a 128-mile trail that loops through the Himalayas. Although Kim felt prepared for the trek, it was still a major undertaking.

"I already had everything I needed to backpack, but we were going to Nepal," Kim says. "We didn't speak the language, we didn't know anybody, and there was no way to contact anyone. You can't just cruise to a hospital if you break your ankle."

Once she landed in Katmandu, Kim negotiated the frenetic city streets and met up with Carlisle at a traveler's hotel. The next day, they obtained hiking permits for the Himalayas and hired a pair of

Sherpas, native people known for their skills in mountaineering, to porter their heavy backpacks.

Kim's Sherpa, Pasang, was quiet, cheerful, and carried an enormous English dictionary in his backpack. His brother was a Sherpa on Everest. Carlisle's Sherpa wore flip-flops instead of hiking boots, and strapped Carlisle's backpack to his head.

The group set off on the Annapurna Circuit, ascending into the desolate foothills of the Himalayas. Each day that they gained elevation, the landscape became more rugged.

"We just walked and walked, and all of a sudden it looked like we were in the high desert," Kim says. "In the distance, there were these gigantic white peaks, and that's where we were going."

As the geography changed, so did the culture. "We were in Buddhist country. There were carvings in the rocks on the trail, prayer flags, and it was quiet, so quiet," Kim remembers. Occasionally, Kim and Carlisle encountered nomads, herds of long-haired yaks, or scrappy donkeys bedecked in tinkling bells and red yarn ornaments.

After two weeks of trekking, Kim and Carlisle reached the village of Manang at 11,545 feet. At this tiny Buddhist outpost packed with stone buildings and goat herds, Kim and Carlisle spent two nights acclimating for the most challenging section of their trip. They were preparing for the trek over Thorong La Pass, which, at 17,769 feet, was the highest point of the Annapurna Circuit.

The pair rose before dawn to begin their trek, layering on every piece of clothing they had for protection from the frigid air, and started up the long, winding trail.

"I felt great," Kim says. "I was so happy because we were getting closer and closer to those big white peaks, which I had been dreaming about my whole life. It was a dream come true."

The women were making good progress, slowly climbing closer to the legendary Himalayan pass.

"Then, at about 16,500 feet in elevation, I started feeling kind of sad. My eyes started watering and I was seeing rainbow halos and sunspots," she says.

Kim Wyatt ascends 17,769-foot Thorong La Pass in Nepal while struggling with altitude sickness.

Kim assumed she was merely emotional, overcome by the majesty of the Himalayas. She didn't know that she was suffering from interocular pressure caused by the high elevation. "I just thought I was crying. I didn't realize it was related to altitude," Kim recalls.

This is how altitude sickness strikes most people—without them realizing it. They might suddenly feel confused, disoriented, or somewhat depressed. They may develop a severe headache or have difficulty catching their breath. But it's easy to write off these symptoms when you're hiking up a steep mountain. You assume that you're just weary from exertion.

Kim had climbed several 14,000-foot peaks in her lifetime, so she hadn't expected that altitude would be a problem. She forged ahead, and as she neared the summit, her condition worsened. Her stride turned into a sluggish walk, then a feeble shuffle. "I was thinking, 'I need to take my time and take it easy,'" she remembers. "But then, I started feeling like I really couldn't walk anymore."

Carlisle had outpaced her friend and was far ahead when she finally looked back and noticed Kim doubled-over and panting. Carlisle asked if she was okay.

Kim was a long way from okay. She was disoriented and on the verge of hyperventilating. "I didn't even know what was going on."

Carlisle could see that Kim was in serious trouble, so she tried to convince her to turn back. But Kim was determined to reach the top. After all, she had traveled so far to get here.

"I knew we were so close. I wasn't going to turn around," Kim says.

So Carlisle walked alongside Kim and coached her through each step. "She'd count to ten, and I would take one step," Kim says. "Then she'd count to ten again, and I would take another step."

With Carlisle at her side and the Sherpas bringing up the rear, Kim inched toward the summit. "I thought I was going to die. I really thought I was never going to see my family again—that this was the end for me," she says.

At one point, Kim collapsed on a mound of loose rocks near the trail, gasping for breath. "I was leaning on this pile of rocks, and Carlisle said, 'Okay, let's step away now.' Later, she told me it was a man's grave. I realized that it must have been someone in my predicament, and that I would not have been the first to perish on that mountain."

Kim's fears were not unfounded. The stones marked the hastily made grave of twenty-seven-year-old Richard James Allen, who had succumbed to altitude sickness on Thorong La Pass in 1991. A small hand-carved plaque inscribed with the warning "Travelers Beware" was placed on top of the rock cairn.

Kim and Carlisle continued trudging onward until finally they reached the highest point of the Annapurna Circuit. Thousands of colorful prayer flags, strung around sharp boulders, fluttered softly in the cold air. A sign read: *Congratulations on your success. Hope you enjoyed the trek.*

A sense of wonder washed over Kim. "It was freezing, but I could see mountains that never stopped, endless vistas of white peaks all the way to Tibet. It was amazing."

The two women reveled in their accomplishment as they rested at the top of Thorong La Pass. "It was a once-in-a-lifetime thing," Kim says. "But I was still totally out of it. There was a little shack selling hot tea, so Carlisle gave me a drink, and then we scooted down the hill."

As the two women descended, Kim's senses slowly came back to her. The lower she went, the better she felt.

"That's when I realized I had gone over my limit in altitude—that my limit is about 16,000 feet and I can't go any higher than that," she says.

Kim suffered no long-term effects from her bout with altitude sickness and says she doesn't regret her decision to keep going. But she says she'd do things differently in the future.

"I don't know how I made it over the pass, but I feel like I almost lost my life doing it. If I were to experience altitude sickness again, if I started to feel that pressure and sluggishness, I would go back down immediately," Kim notes.

Her take-home lesson for all other hikers: "Know your limits. I know mine now."

***

Altitude sickness, also known as acute mountain sickness, is a silent and mysterious predator. Most people associate it with high mountainous regions like Nepal, but the fact is that it can affect hikers at elevations as low as 8,000 feet, a common elevation in the mountainous areas of the United States. Above 8,000 feet, there is a noticeably lower amount of oxygen in the air we breathe. The barometric pressure is also reduced. This is why airplanes that fly above 8,000 feet have pressurized cabins, in which the air pressure is mechanically regulated. If not, passengers would get sick on every flight, with symptoms ranging from what feels like a mild hangover—headache, nausea, fatigue—to more serious conditions like vomiting and fainting.

Hikers can't easily control their own barometric pressure. In Kim Wyatt's case, she was suffering from a fairly acute case of altitude sickness. If she had stayed at 17,769-foot Thorong La Pass much longer, her condition would have likely worsened. Anyone feeling as bad as Kim did is showing the warning signs of not just altitude sickness, but its much more serious next step: HAPE (excess fluid in the lungs) or HACE (fluid in the brain). Both HAPE and HACE can be fatal within hours—which is why every year people die of altitude sickness even though it's completely preventable. When there is excess fluid in a hiker's lungs (HAPE), he or she experiences breathlessness even at rest, and this is a very bad sign. Even at the top of Mount Everest, a climber should not feel breathless while sitting still. When there is fluid in a hiker's brain (HACE), he or she will be mumbling, confused, and stumbling. HAPE and HACE often occur simultaneously.

But preventing all of this trouble is a no-brainer. Any person experiencing altitude sickness in any form—mild, moderate, or even severe—can mitigate the problem by heading downhill. Unfortunately, most people experiencing altitude sickness don't have the

In the Sierra Nevada and Rocky Mountains, many trails rise above 10,000 feet, so altitude preparation matters.

presence of mind to do so. Like Kim, they will be so focused on their goal—whether it's climbing Mount Whitney at 14,505 feet or gaining the summit of Thorong La Pass in Nepal—and so muddled in their reasoning that they refuse to turn back.

The problem is compounded by the fact that it's extremely difficult to predict who will be affected. It's not uncommon for healthy, athletic people to have a tougher time at high elevations than their unfit companions. This may be partly because physically fit people are more inclined to push themselves. They might get up at the crack of dawn at their sea-level home, drive a few hours to the mountains, and then in the early afternoon, start hiking up an 8,000-foot peak at a fast clip. They haven't considered the fact that they are pushing their lungs through an 8,000-foot elevation change in only half a day. One of the golden rules of altitude sickness is that the faster you ascend, the more likely you are to get sick. That sea-level dweller would be better off driving to the mountains, sleeping one night at 6,000 feet, then climbing the 8,000-foot peak the following day—and taking their sweet time, not racing up the trail.

Two factors will greatly decrease your chances of getting altitude sickness: giving your body plenty of time to adjust to the altitude, and hiking slowly. The body has an amazing ability to acclimatize, but adequate time is the key. Conventional wisdom says that it takes about a week for the body to adapt to 16,000-foot elevation. Kim spent a few nights acclimatizing at 11,000 feet in Manang, but then she added an extra 6,000 feet heading up to Thorong La Pass. For her, that difference was too great. For her friend, it wasn't. Kim had been at 14,000 feet many times without any problems, but that didn't guarantee her success at 17,000 feet.

Altitude Sickness Takeaways

1. It takes a full seventy-two hours to acclimate to major elevation changes, although many people acclimate fairly well after only twenty-four to forty-eight hours. The best preparation for hiking at a high elevation is to sleep at that elevation, or as close to

it as possible, the night before. If you are planning a strenuous hike at 7,000 feet or above, spend a day or two prior doing easier hikes at the same elevation. Also, get plenty of rest and drink plenty of water. Lack of sleep and drinking alcohol can contribute to "feeling the altitude."

2. If you've never hiked above a certain elevation—say 13,000 feet—you don't know how you are going to feel until you get there. If you start to feel ill (nausea, vomiting, severe headache or the like), you are experiencing altitude sickness. Some people can get by with taking an aspirin and trudging onward, but if you are seriously ill, the only cure is to descend as soon as possible. If the altitude has gotten to you badly enough, you may need someone to help you walk. Fatigue and elevation sickness can cloud your judgment in the same manner hypothermia does, so take action before your symptoms become too severe.

3. If you're hiking with companions, pay close attention to how they are feeling at higher elevations. They may not recognize their own symptoms of altitude sickness, especially if they are suffering from disorientation, as in Kim Wyatt's case. It's up to you to notice your hiking partner's symptoms and lead him or her back downhill if necessary. You can always summit the peak on another day.

Hiking with Dogs

Dogs are wonderful friends and great companions. We love to hike with our dogs, and our dogs love us for it. But dogs and wilderness do not always mix well. Bless their furry little hearts, most dogs can't help but disturb wildlife by barking at squirrels or chasing deer. That's why it's up to dog owners to carefully control their dogs in the wilderness—whether by leash or voice control. Pay close attention to your dog on the trail, and he or she can be the best hiking companion you could ask for. Don't pay close attention, and disasters can happen.

Here's a general guideline to park rules about dogs: if you are visiting a national park like Yosemite or the Grand Canyon or Yellowstone, your dog will not be allowed to hike with you on the vast majority of park trails. Dogs are permitted in most campgrounds and picnic areas, but they are not allowed on hiking trails. There are only a very few exceptions to this rule within the national park system. The dog kennel in Yosemite Valley is a terribly sad place where dog owners who don't know the no-dogs-on-national-park-trails rule board their canines. The owners head off for fantastic hikes to Yosemite Falls or Half Dome while their dogs sit glumly in cages, wondering what they did wrong.

If you are planning to visit a national park, consider leaving your dog at home with a friend, or take him or her to one of those chic dog hotels. After all, your furry friend deserves the best.

In national forest or wilderness lands, dogs are usually permitted off-leash, except in special wildlife management areas or other special-use areas. Your dog should still be under voice control, however. Nature presents many hazards for dogs, including coyotes, mountain lions, black bears, skunks, porcupines, ticks, rattlesnakes, and a host of other potential problems. Dogs can get lost, too. A dog who runs off to chase a deer or a coyote or even a rabbit may travel so far in unfamiliar terrain that he or she can't find you again. Some dogs will take off running if a thunderstorm strikes. Keeping your dog close to your side or on a leash will help you both have a worry-free trip and a great time.

At other types of parks (state, county, regional, etc.), dogs may or may not be allowed on hiking trails. The rules vary widely from one park to another, so always find out the park's specific rules before you decide to bring your dog there. Often, if dogs are allowed, they must be on a six-foot or shorter leash. Don't try to get away with carrying the leash in your hand while your dog runs free; rangers may give you a ticket.

Search-and-rescue expert Lisa Whatford has spent most of twenty-five years working with search-and-rescue dogs, so we asked her to give us her best tips for taking care of your pooch on hikes. Here are some of her recommendations:

1. Teach your dog to lay down in creeks and swim in water. That will help him or her maintain good body temperature on long hikes.

A well-trained dog can carry his or her own pack on multi-day trips.

2. Dark-colored dogs absorb light and can overheat quickly. They need more water and shade and are susceptible to overheating. If a dog starts shade-hopping on a hike, that means it needs water to drink and lay down in, and a break to cool down.

3. Like humans, dogs can collapse and die of heat exhaustion. If a dog's tongue is enlarged and hanging out, it's a sign of overheating. Take steps to cool down your dog immediately. Remember that your dog is probably going to be much hotter than you are, first because she is wearing a fur coat, but second because she is a lot closer to the ground than you are. The heat that is reflecting off the trail is only a few inches from her belly. Meanwhile you're enjoying the fresh air and cool breeze from five or six feet higher.

4. Be wary of dogs near fast moving water. Dogs don't have good depth perception. Don't assume a dog can easily cross logs or bridges with fast moving water underneath them. These are learned skills that don't come naturally.

5. The same goes for boulder fields, where the dog needs to hop from boulder to boulder. Dogs can freeze in fear just like us. They need to learn agility; they aren't necessarily born with it.

6. If you're hiking through challenging terrain, you can put a light harness on your dog to help her through the steepest and rockiest areas, or help her cross log bridges.

7. Trim you dog's toenails. If his nails are too long, he can't have good traction with his pads. It can be very painful, like hiking in high heels. Plus it makes dogs prone to getting a broken or torn nail, which is very bad.

8. Always carry a minimum of one bootie in case your dog has a foot injury. A dog's pad can easily get cut on rocky trails or burned on extremely hot terrain.

9. Carry water specifically for your dog, in addition to your own water for you. Don't count on finding streams or lakes or springs for your dog to drink out of. Always have a backup. We like to carry plastic foldable bowls for our dogs, so they don't have to drink out of our water bottles. We have a couple of bowls made by Orikaso and Fozzils that weigh almost nothing and fold flat, so they don't take up any space in our packs.

10. Carry dog poop bags so you can relocate your dog's poop. Don't leave it on the trail.

Packs for Your Pooch

If you're going backpacking with your dog, he or she can do some of the work. With a proper dog pack that is weighted and balanced correctly, most dogs will happily carry a modest amount of weight. Our dogs always carry their own dog food, plus their leashes (if they aren't wearing them). Mature dogs can carry about 20 percent of their body weight; younger dogs should carry a bit less. As the trip moves on and our dogs eat their food, we fill their packs with the trash we want to pack out. Trash usually weighs less than dog food, so the dogs' packs naturally get lighter as the trip wears on.

Dog packs have two nylon pouches that fit over a dog's back—one pack for each side of the dog—plus a strap that goes around the dog's belly and another that goes across his chest. The contraption is similar to a horse's packsaddle. The pouches are suspended over the dog's flanks in a way that should not chafe its legs or sides.

Make sure the weight in your pooch's pack is evenly balanced.

The most important element in packing your dog's pack is making sure that the weight is evenly distributed on both sides, so your dog's balance isn't compromised. It's easy to tell if the pack is off-balance because it will "droop" on one side of your dog. Most dogs will act a bit strange the first time you put a pack on them, but in about five minutes they get used to it and trot along without a care in the world.

We always pack our dogs' food in waterproof Ziploc bags inside their packs, so that when they dash into a stream to cool off, they don't drench their food. Wet dog food is a lot heavier to carry than dry dog food.

Hiking Psychology

When you're out in the wilderness, your relationships with the people around you take on a much larger significance than they do in the suburbs or city. After all, the people you hike with—or even the strangers you pass on the trail or meet on a mountain summit—may be the people with whom you share your most memorable moments. They might also be the people who get you into deep doo-doo. Or they may be the ones who save your butt when you need a rescue. No matter which way it goes, in the backcountry, relationships count. It's worth sharing a few stories about the complexity of human interaction in the wilderness.

Don't Split Up

In early summer of 2011, David Orr went on a casual day hike with his two friends, Adam and Nick, in Desolation Wilderness, a sprawling hiker's playground near Lake Tahoe, California. Halfway through their stroll, they decided it would be fun to summit 9,735-foot Mt. Tallac, which loomed above them.

"We thought it couldn't be that far to the top," David says, "but we didn't investigate what the hike was like." The three friends glanced at the trail map, and decided that the nearly 10,000-foot peak would be an easy side-trip.

They trekked toward the mountain, but the farther they climbed, the more difficult the trail became. "I remember being intimidated by the landscape," David recalls. "It wasn't a dirt trail like I was used to. There were lots of granite boulders and sharp, loose stones from rockslides."

David and his friends were from the San Francisco Bay Area, which is 7,000 feet lower in elevation than the lowlands of Desolation Wilderness. "We didn't anticipate how tired we'd get from the altitude. It was really tough," he says. He wore Vibram FiveFingers shoes and carried a small Camelbak of water with a few snacks shoved in its pockets.

As they climbed the trail higher towards Mt. Tallac's summit, the men ran out of water. "It was hot and we were sweating and none of us rationed our water. We just kept drinking till it was gone," David says.

Luckily, Adam had stashed iodine water-purifying pills in his pack. "At every stream we came across, we'd refill our Camelbaks and drop an iodine pill into them, so we were drinking this really terrible tasting water," David says.

The three friends pushed forward, climbing up the sliding, rock-strewn face of the mountain. "We made it to the point where we were only about 200 feet from the top, but by the time we got there, we were haggard and tired," David remembers. "I had pushed myself too hard and was feeling really out of it. I had completely run out of juice."

Nick seemed to be in even worse shape. He decided to sit and rest while David and Adam scrambled to the summit. When they reached the top, David felt elated. "It was like being on top of the world. Mt. Tallac is one of the tallest peaks in the area, and you can see 360 degrees in every direction."

The two lounged on the top of the mountain, soaking up the last rays of the afternoon sun. After resting a while, they heaved themselves to their feet and picked their way back down the slope to meet up with Nick. "But when we got to the bottom, he was nowhere to be found," David says. "We looked at each other and knew this was not good. We had no idea what direction he might have gone.

He could have been anywhere. He could have been at the bottom of the trailhead waiting for us. We didn't know what to do."

To make matters worse, David and Adam knew that Nick is severely nearsighted. He could have easily missed a trail junction or taken a wrong turn.

"Adam left to climb to a higher point and look for him. While he was doing that, I finally received a text," David says. He took photos of where he was and sent them to Nick, who texted back photos of the landscape surrounding him. "We started to orient ourselves and I realized Nick had wandered off-trail and right off the back of the mountain."

David and Adam hiked down to where they believed Nick had gone. "We had to walk off the back of Mt. Tallac to try to reach him. Once we found him, we had to hike all the way back up."

Happily reunited, the three friends slogged back to the trail. "By this time, I had nothing left in me," David says. He looked at the trail that wound through the steep, rocky scree below him and realized, "I still had to hike halfway down the mountain, about six miles."

Since they'd lost so much time, David suggested a shortcut. "I just wanted to get home. It was late in the day, and I thought it would save some time."

He left his friends and tried to descend cross-country across a lingering snowfield. Almost instantly he lost control of his footing and tumbled down the steep slope, landing in a pile of rocks. The whole right side of his body was shredded and bloody. His Vibram FiveFingers had done nothing to protect his feet from the impact. "My left foot had hit something hard. My big toe was stuck and pointed in the wrong direction," David says.

David howled in pain as Adam pulled his shoe off. "Instantly my foot got really swollen," David recounts. "We forced the shoe back on because I had to hike out of Desolation Wilderness on a broken foot."

It took a grueling six hours, much of it in darkness, to get back to their car. They made it, but all three men were exhausted and dehydrated.

Since that trip, David has gained a lot of backcountry knowledge. "We made one mistake after another on that day," he says. The men bit off more than they could chew by setting off for the mountain summit without investigating how difficult the hike would be. They were hiking in a group, but they didn't stay together, and one of their members wound up lost. They were woefully unprepared for the physical demands of their trip, which led them to make poor decisions, and that led to David's broken foot.

"Being properly prepared is important, even for a day hike," David notes. Now he always carries lots of extra food and emergency items. And he also studies the map carefully before he decides to take any "easy side-trips," even if a mountain summit is calling his name. Most importantly, he knows that he has to hike smart not just for himself but also for his friends, so no one gets left behind.

What We Can Learn

Search-and-rescue experts Lisa Whatford and Chris Kozlowski work a lot of rescue missions on the Mount Tallac Trail, where David and his friends ran into trouble. They say that what happened to the men is fairly typical of the kinds of problems day hikers encounter, especially in popular tourist areas like Lake Tahoe.

"Most of the time we're not searching for day hikers, we're just rescuing them. They hiked too far, they weren't prepared, they got exhausted and they just sat down on the trail and called 911 on their cell phones," Lisa says. "These kinds of hikers are usually easy to find because they're sitting right next to the trail, but they're in bad shape because they're depleted or dehydrated or feeling bad from the altitude."

When hiking in groups, she advises the following: "Don't split up. One reason we have to go find lost hikers is because one person is hiking slower than the other person, and they'll say, 'Go ahead, I'll meet you there.' The slower person never shows up, they get lost on the way, and no one's there to help them find their way. You're only as fast as your weakest link. Don't leave your companion. Don't separate. A lot of our searches happen that way. If you are hiking with other people, take care of each other and look after each other."

Choose Your Hiking Partner Wisely

If it hasn't happened already, some day you'll be out there with one of those hikers who says, "It'll be quicker if we head straight down off the ridge." When you hear those words, remember Suzanne Roberts's story.

By the time Suzanne was twenty-three, she was already an experienced hiker. She had completed the world-famous 211-mile John Muir Trail in the Sierra Nevada Mountains, so she wasn't daunted by the prospect of a week-long backpacking trip in Lake Tahoe's Desolation Wilderness. She planned the trip with her boyfriend, Jack, and a college buddy, Jason.

"Jack and I met up with Jason to hike from Emerald Bay to Echo Lakes along the Tahoe Rim Trail. We had been out for a few days already, and we planned to camp one more night on the other side of Dick's Pass," Suzanne says.

As the three hikers started over the pass, Jason noticed a faint trail up Dick's Peak. He suggested they drop their peaks and climb the peak. "I felt a little nervous because of the snow," Suzanne says. "But Jason said, 'We'll follow the rocks on the ridgeline. We can mostly avoid the snow that way.'"

"We dropped our packs and pulled out water, food, and rain gear to bring with us. Then we started up the boulders. Jason went first, testing each rock for stability, calling to Jack and me if anything seemed wonky. Climbing up the ridge proved slow going, but we reached the peak in about an hour. We took pictures and admired the view, and then we decided we'd better head down because clouds were building."

"That's when Jack said that hiking the ridgeline was too slow. He wanted us to go down the rocks, which were covered with snow. 'I'm going to slide down,' he said. 'It'll be way faster and fun.'"

Suzanne and Jason told Jack that sliding down the icy slope seemed like a bad idea. Even though they were hiking in July, a white swath clung to the rocks and fanned out into a huge pile of sharp boulders. They did everything possible to convince him not to do it.

"It was so steep that even our dog Dylan whined at the top," Suzanne remembers. "He was the type of dog who takes risks, but even he wouldn't step on that snow. Jack kept saying that it would be fine. He pulled his rain gear out of his day-pack and put it on so he would slide faster."

Jack crawled sideways onto the snowfield, and almost immediately, "he lost his grip and started sliding sideways down the slope. He fell like a rag doll for about fifty yards, his arms and legs thrashing. He gripped at the snow but his flailing body kept tumbling down. We just stood there, watching. There was nothing we could do."

Jack finally crashed into the rocks at the bottom and lay still between two boulders. "Jason and I made our way down the rocks as quickly as we could. When we finally reached Jack, he wasn't moving. Jason, who was studying to be a doctor, thought Jack was going into shock. He put his jacket over Jack and raised his legs, and then Jack seemed to pull out of it," she says.

"Finally, Jason tried to get Jack to walk, and he could limp a little. We redistributed Jack's pack so he didn't have to carry much weight, and we made it down to a nearby lake to spend the night." The next day, the group aborted the rest of their trip and hiked out early. Jack was in rough shape, but he was able to hike slowly to the trailhead. Not long afterward, he had to have surgery on his knee.

What We Can Learn

Suzanne remembers how disgusted she was with her boyfriend's recklessness: "His decision to slide down that snow cut our trip short. It was totally selfish. I was young at the time and the only woman in the group, so I think it was harder for me to make the rules. But I'm not like that anymore. If someone is doing something that's going to jeopardize our trip, I speak up."

"It's stressful to hike with people who take too many chances. Choose your hiking partners very, very carefully. Just because you're having sex with someone doesn't mean you should go hiking with them."

Know When to Turn Around

Here's another cautionary tale from sixty-eight-year-old hiker Mason Brutschy. Mason was a twenty-year-old junior at UC Berkeley when this sobering event occurred. "This is the only time I've ever been really lost in the Sierra or spent a night out in the Sierra with no tent or tarp or sleeping bag," he says.

Mason and a group of college-age friends worked at a summer camp on Bass Lake, south of Yosemite National Park, and spent their days off exploring the surrounding wilderness. Right before Labor Day weekend, the group left Florence Lake and backpacked for two days up to Evolution Valley, where they set up camp.

"The next day, most of our group decided to hike around the valley and visit the hot springs at Blaney Meadow, but I wanted to climb Mount Darwin," he says.

The distinct flat-topped summit of this peak pokes through the clouds at 13,831 feet; it's a Sierra icon that winds up on many peak enthusiasts' lists.

"I left camp early with a lady named Casey Boyle, who was going to be a senior at UC Davis. We left early in the morning and hiked up into the granite and the snow. At about 1 p.m., she got tired of climbing and decided to sit and wait for me. I was young and energetic, and I continued up. It took me until 3:30 to get to the top—and that should have been a warning sign right there. But it was a fabulous view.

Mason started down from the summit, and around 5 p.m. he met up with Casey. The two of them continued downhill, but they were both tired and moving slowly.

"We started hiking down the main chute to Evolution Valley and it started getting dark. We wound our way down, but it was completely dark by the time we got into the valley. It was probably 8 at night. I had no idea where to find our camp, so I yelled out one or two times to see if our friends would answer. Nobody did. It was getting cold, and there was no moon that night. Casey started crying and saying 'Oh God, we're lost.'

"There are a lot of wet meadows in Evolution Valley, and we tried slogging around trying to find the trail, but I couldn't get my bearings in the dark. It seemed like there were a lot of trees, and we couldn't see a thing. So I said, 'Let's just stop. We're not getting anywhere. Let's spend the night here against a tree. We'll huddle together for warmth.'

"We spent the night huddled near a tree. I put my arms around Casey and did what I could to keep her warm. I remember she cried a lot. We were wearing only T-shirts and shorts, and it probably got down to 35 or 40 degrees that night. But we were young and we made it through."

The next morning the sky got light around 6 a.m. Mason and Casey got up and could see the trail. Even when they reached it, they still weren't sure which way to go, so they just sat down on the trail and yelled for their friends. Sure enough, about a half-hour later, their friends came up the trail and got them.

What We Can Learn

The biggest takeaway from this story is to avoid being too goal-oriented. Don't be so focused on getting to your destination that you take unnecessary risks, like leaving your slower partner behind and bagging the summit way too late in the day. Know when to call it a day and admit that you can't do what you planned on doing—or at least not before it gets dark. Mason claims that "the moral of this story is that 2 o'clock is always the turnaround time. If we're not there by 2, we need to turn back. There will always be another day to climb Mount Darwin." Turn around by 2 and you'll always be able to find your way back to camp in the daylight.

Search-and-rescue expert Lisa Whatford says that the biggest problem that hikers can face is darkness. "You didn't realize it would take so long and you don't have a headlamp, and you can't see the trail anymore. And then we get the 911 call. A lot of times hikers underestimate how long a hike is going to take. The simplest thing is to check your watch when you start. If you go out and hike for two

To make sure you're back at camp before dark, plan on a strict turnaround time for peak climbs and other adventures.

hours, figure it's going to take another two hours to get back. Do you still have two hours of daylight left? It's common sense, but people forget that basic thing."

One other lesson to learn from this story regards preparedness. Mason and Casey would have had a much more comfortable night if they'd brought a few basic essentials with them: warm layers, headlamp or flashlight, matches, food, water filter, etc. Never go out for a day hike assuming that you will make it back before dark. Every once in a while, you won't. Fortunately, Mason was smart enough to stop the downward spiral of events. The pair hunkered down and did their best to stay warm until dawn. If they kept wandering around in the dark, they might have gotten even wetter and colder, or worse yet, injured. Their decision to stay put until daylight most likely saved them from a much worse predicament.

3
Boots, Blisters, and Foot Care

Choosing the Right Boots

You might wonder why an entire chapter of this book is devoted to feet. Here's why: every hiker eventually conducts a search for the perfect shoe. For some, it becomes the eternal quest. They continue that search for most of their lives, their finicky feet never feeling totally satisfied.

The question we're asked more than any other is, "What kind of boots do you wear?" The answer? It doesn't really matter since those same boots may not work well for you. Feet are remarkably unique. Every hiker has to figure out what works for the peculiarities and irregularities of his or her feet. And that will probably take some trial and error.

Ann Marie has arthritis in her right great toe (the technical term for the big one). She has six metal pins and a plate in her right ankle, which sometimes rub painfully against her shoes. She's also had some Achilles' heel problems. In short, her feet are a mess. They would probably qualify for federal disaster relief.

If she added up all the money she's spent on hiking shoes and boots during her lifetime, she'd have a nice down payment on a house, or at least a swanky mobile home. But despite her high-maintenance feet, she manages to hike fifteen- to twenty-mile days on a regular basis, even while carrying a heavy pack. The key is paying attention to her feet, treating them kindly, and finding the right shoes to make them comfortable.

A vast number of websites are devoted to testing out different kinds of hiking shoes and boots. To that we say, "Whatever." If you talk to people who hike a lot—more than once or twice a week—most will agree that it's not the brand or model of the boot that matters, but the fit and the weight. Fit relates to the shape of a particular shoe's last, or, in other words, the template from which it is made. Your foot's "fit" may be wider in the toes, narrower in the ankle, wider in the mid-foot, etc. You have to find a hiking shoe that matches your particular foot. This may involve some trial and error, or at least a lot of time spent trying on shoes.

Weight is a simpler matter to address because every manufacturer lists the weight of its shoes in its specifications. The ancient, wizened hiker's adage says that "an extra pound on your feet is like five on your back," and even though we're not ancient or wizened, we agree with that. Our long-distance thru-hiker friends—people who hike thousands of miles on the Pacific Crest Trail, the Continental Divide Trail, or the Appalachian Trail—wear lightweight trail running shoes, not heavy leather hiking boots. Their goal is to wear shoes that lead to the least amount of foot fatigue. Keep the weight off your feet and you'll hike faster and farther.

We're not saying this is the perfect recipe for everyone. We're saying that it works for a lot of people, including ourselves. The fact is that it's possible to hike in seriously challenging terrain in almost any kind of comfortable footwear that has some sort of rubberized sole and a modicum of comfort. What the heck, we once saw a woman on top of Half Dome who was wearing gold lamé sandals. Was she helicoptered to the top? We could never figure it out, but there she was.

Well-constructed trail running shoes or hiking shoes will last a lot longer than Converse hightops or tennis shoes. They will also provide much better traction on steep descents lined with loose decomposed

Rocky trails require sturdy footwear, but not necessarily heavy leather boots.

granite—DG, as hikers call it—which acts like ball bearings under your feet. Big, heavy boots are not necessarily the best choice, even though a lot of newbies feel compelled to buy them.

What about ankle support? That's probably the biggest concern hikers express about wearing lightweight trail runners versus heavy leather hiking boots. However, multiple studies at the University of Massachusetts and University of Southern California have shown that strengthening ligaments and tendons and stretching ankles are better ways to prevent ankle injury than wearing heavy boots.

A long-distance hiking friend finally gave up his heavy leather boots five years ago. He always thought he had to wear them because he was prone to ankle sprains from his college years as a basketball player. Now he wears lightweight trail runners, but because he's nervous about ankle support, he also wears a fabric compression brace on both ankles. He hasn't had an ankle problem since he switched shoes, and he's walked upwards of 4,000 trail miles since then.

By cutting down on the burden of weight on your feet, you're also protecting your knees, joints, and bones. Foot fatigue leads to missteps, falls, and twisted ankles.

It's true that trail runners or lightweight hiking boots won't last as long as hardcore mountain boots will last. Your lightweight shoes may compress or wear out after only 300 miles or so, depending on your weight, hiking style, and the terrain you're walking on. Rocky trails are hard on shoes, and there isn't anything you can do about that. But because lightweight hikers and trail running shoes usually cost much less than heavy boots, your net cash outlay for shoes probably won't be any larger. You might spend $70 to $120 on lightweight shoes, and twice that much on leather mountaineering boots. So what if you replace the lightweight pair twice a year?

If you're shopping for lightweight shoes, look for thick soles, so you won't feel rocks through them. Many runners wear minimalist shoes, which have very thin soles so they can feel the ground under their feet. The minimalist idea works great on fairly level surfaces, but on a bumpy, rocky trail, it's good to have some cushion between your feet and the ground. The heavier your backpack, the more shoe cushion you'll want.

Also, while zero-drop or barefoot-style shoes are extremely popular, they aren't the best solution for everybody. There's a correlation between zero-drop shoes (shoes that have no elevation difference between the forefoot and the heel) and athletes with heel problems, both plantar fasciitis and Achilles' tendinopathy. Zero-drop shoes seem to work pretty well for level walking, but not so well for hills. Think about the geometry of climbing a steep slope: You have to lean forward slightly to keep from falling backward, which requires your foot muscles to engage. If you're barefoot, you'll have to balance on your toes and forefoot, or else dig in hard with your entire foot, especially your heel, to keep your balance. That's how heel problems can develop. If you wear shoes with a modicum of elevation (maybe nine or ten mm drop instead of zero), your heel is already lifted slightly as you walk uphill, and you don't have to lean so hard to stay balanced.

If you decide to hike in running shoes, make sure you buy trail-running shoes, not road-running shoes. The difference is in the traction. Examine the bottom of the soles—you want a shoe with aggressive lugs that will give you solid purchase on granite and mud. Ann Marie prefers lugs of at least five millimeters because she has small feet and likes the feel of extra grippy-ness. Lugs wear down quickly on rocky trails, so those five millimeters wear down to three millimeters pretty fast. Some lightweight shoes have sticky rubber on the outsole to provide friction on slippery terrain.

Another factor you'll hear bandied about is the shape of the footbed. We've come a long way in understanding how feet work, and many podiatrists now believe the best clues can be found in a baby's feet. Ever notice how a baby's cute little toes are the widest part of his or her foot? Unlike adult feet, which have been shoved into shoes for a number of years, baby feet hold their natural shape,

Hiking footwear choices left to right: leather hiking boots, light-weight hiking shoes, and trail running shoes.

which is basically a V-shape. The heel is at the bottom and the toes at the top of the V. Adult feet tend to be more rectangular shaped; that is, the toes are about the same width as the rest of the foot. That's not the way Mother Nature intended it to be. Even worse, adult toes often lean in toward each other or even cross over each other. They've been crammed into confining shoes for far too long.

Now, in light of this issue, shoe companies are coming out with athletic shoes that are shaped a bit like clown shoes, with a wide toe box and narrow heel. To this we say, "Hallelujah!" For a vast majority of hikers, the single most important factor to look for in hiking shoes is a wide toe box. Toes don't want to be fenced in. Crammed toes lead to foot injuries and blisters. Give those little piggies some room to move around, and your entire gait will change. You'll hike more efficiently and comfortably.

So, what shoes do we wear? Our current favorites in lightweight hiking shoes are several different models made by the shoe companies Keen, Merrell, and Sportiva. In trail running shoes, which we often wear for hiking, we like the ROCLITE shoes from the British company inov-8. All three of these brands appeal to us for the same reasons—wide toe box, thick lugs, solid gripping performance, and ultralight weight.

At the Store

Finding the right hiking shoe requires a lot of shopping. To make this chore easier, start by going at the right time of day. What? Yup, timing matters. Try on hiking shoes at the end of the day, when your feet are enlarged. That way you won't wind up with boots that are too small. Make sure you wear the socks that you usually wear for hiking (more info on socks coming up later in this chapter). The thickness of your socks can radically alter a boot's fit. Ditto for orthotics. If you can't walk a mile without your $400 custom orthotics, make sure you put them inside every hiking shoe you try on, and see how they feel.

In terms of sizing, try on hiking shoes (or trail runners) that are a half-size larger than the shoes you normally wear to work. You want to have a "scooch" more room than what you're accustomed to in your day-to-day shoes. In sandals and heels, Terra wears a size 8. But in hiking shoes and trail runners, she wears a size 8.5.

Ask yourself: Is there enough room in the toe box so that your toes can spread or wiggle slightly, especially when hiking downhill? If any of your toes touch the front of your boots, count on blisters. Most outdoors stores have inclined platforms for testing out hiking shoes. Walk down the slope several times. Do your toes push forward and touch the boot front? Go bigger. As you hike, your feet spread and flatten out. You want shoes that will feel as good after fifteen miles as they do when you first put them on.

Another consideration when buying lightweight hikers or trail running shoes is whether to go waterproof or not. Waterproof shoes usually have been treated with Gore-tex or a similar product, and, in theory, this seems like a good idea. Your shoes won't get wet, right? Wrong. Often when your hiking shoes get wet, it's raining. Or you've just walked through a stream. In either case, water is going to come in through the tops of your shoes, around your ankle, so it doesn't matter if the shoe sides are waterproof. Not only that, but waterproof shoes tend to be heavier. They also tend to make your feet feel hotter—like they are stuffed into a prison cell—whereas shoes with mesh or fabric sides will keep your feet cooler. Hot feet are a recipe for blisters. No one wants blisters.

Size Matters

The bottom line: when it comes to shoes, size matters. Bigger is better. Just ask Stephanie Coates. Twenty-year-old Stephanie was never the outdoorsy type until she attended college at Lake Tahoe, a massive alpine lake that straddles California and Nevada. Surrounded by granite peaks and dense pine and fir forests, Tahoe could turn almost anyone into an outdoors junkie.

After her first semester, Stephanie decided to solo hike the Tahoe Rim Trail, a 165-mile loop that circumnavigates Lake Tahoe. Most people take two weeks to hike the entire TRT, averaging a mellow twelve miles per day.

Stephanie had never done a big backpacking trip. She didn't even own a tent. "I had this grand plan to hike 165 miles by myself, and I had only ever hiked twenty miles over one weekend," she says.

To prepare for the trip, she researched the trail, borrowed backpacking equipment, and bought her first pair of hiking boots. At an outdoors store, Stephanie tried on a pair of boots that she'd researched online. The leather, mid-height boots were designed for durability and support. Stephanie liked them, but was torn over which size to get. Size 10.5 fit snugly and comfortably, and size 11 fit well too, but was a little roomy. She decided to go for snug and bought the 10.5s.

Stephanie knew that she should break-in her boots before she hit the trail. But somehow, she never got around to it. Walking on a treadmill for twenty minutes was the extent of her boot-testing.

Of course you can tell where this story is going.

In July 2015, Stephanie began her solo hike. Less than a couple miles into the journey, her feet began to hurt. "I was sweating like crazy, and my feet were rubbing against the boots," she recalls. She walked another four miles before stopping to camp. When she took off her boots, her feet were swollen and tender. "Only eight miles in, and I was already dying. It felt like my feet had been bound by the hiking boots."

The next morning, Stephanie's feet were even worse. On her heels and in the crannies between her toes, blisters sprouted.

Stephanie wanted to give up and go home, but then it dawned on her that she may have bought the wrong size boots. "I realized I should not be in this much pain," Stephanie remembers. "The boots just weren't right."

She continued down the trail even though every step made her feet throb. She reached her next camp ten miles later. When she pulled off her boots, she saw that "my feet had turned purple and my toenails were black."

Stephanie didn't know what to do. She was determined to complete the TRT, but her feet were in terrible shape. "I thought back on the book *Wild* by Cheryl Strayed. Strayed had the same problem. Her boots were too small," she says. "I realized I had just pulled my own personal Cheryl Strayed."

Stephanie knew that in order to finish her 165-mile trek, she needed new, larger boots. The next day, she hiked thirteen miles and then hopped on a bus that took her into the town of South Lake Tahoe. She checked into a youth hostel, then went to a sporting goods store and bought the exact same pair of boots in a larger size.

"When I tried them on, I realized my toes could actually move, and I thought, this is what boots are supposed to feel like."

Stephanie returned to the TRT the next day, but the pain was still with her. Unlike lightweight hiking shoes or trail runners, leather hiking boots can't be worn right out of the box without some break-in time.

"Now the problem was that my boots weren't broken in. They were so rigid," Stephanie says. "I had blisters, bruised feet, and my toenails were loose. Having to break in new boots when my feet were in that condition hurt worse than when I had boots that were too small."

At this point, Stephanie decided her backpacking adventure was just too miserable. She stopped on the trail and sat down. "I knew I'd screwed up by not preparing. I thought, maybe I'll come back next year when I'm better prepared."

She hiked ten more painful miles, reaching beautiful Star Lake that evening. "The sun was setting, and it looked like a painting," Stephanie remembers. "The mountains were black and the sky was purple, pink and red. It was the most amazing thing I'd ever seen. I didn't even care about my feet anymore."

In a couple more days, Stephanie' new leather boots started to soften up and mold to her feet, and her pain dissipated. She finished her trip—all 165 miles of it—and even though her blackened toenails fell off a few weeks later, she was still proud of her accomplishment. "I'm really glad I stuck it out. I learned so much," she says.

Breaking In Your Boots

As Stephanie learned the hard way, even perfect-fitting boots need to be broken in. That's especially true if you choose to wear sturdy leather boots. But even flexible, lightweight hikers and trail running shoes should go through a break-in period before you rely on them for a long trip. They may feel good right out of the box, but you can only be 100 percent confident about any pair of shoes after you've worn them for several miles. Leather boots can take weeks of wearing before they soften up and form to your feet.

To break in boots, just wear them. Start by wearing them around the house. If you find one of the shoes pinches you in the little toe or has a seam that feels like it's in the wrong spot, you can return your still-clean shoes to the store without any questions asked. If they feel good in the house, then wear them on a trail, but don't start with a twenty-miler. Take your shoes on a five-mile hike, and pay attention to how your feet feel. All good? Okay, now put a heavier pack on your back and take the shoes for another five-miler. Do that a couple more times and you can be sure these shoes will treat your feet well.

Blisters: The Bane of Every Hiker's Existence

The one problem that almost every hiker encounters at one time or another isn't a hungry bear or a sudden snowstorm; it's blisters. Painful blisters are no joke; they can ruin even the most spectacular hike. Even if you have wonderful boots that fit your feet perfectly, you may someday wind up with a blister. Maybe your socks got scrunched up around the toe or the heel, or maybe your shoe had a speck of sand in it. It happens. If you deal with it immediately, it's no big deal. If you don't, it can ruin your trip.

The biggest single reason that people get into blister trouble (besides wearing boots that don't fit) is that they don't pay enough attention to their feet. Our feet are trying to tell us something, but are we listening? We may notice a bit of discomfort but we keep

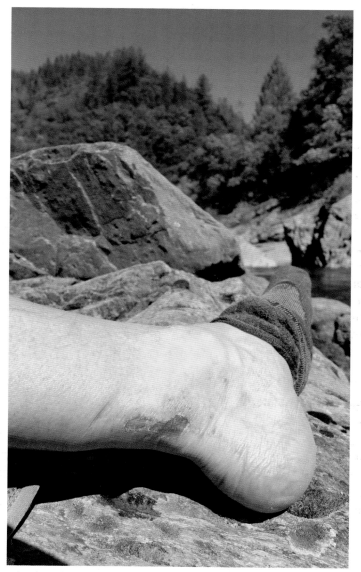

Don't let this happen to you. Untreated blisters can ruin your trip.

on walking, eager to reach our destination. This is a huge mistake. At the slightest indication of pressure or rubbing or heat at any single spot on either foot, you must STOP. Take off your shoe and look at your sock. Is it folding over or scrunching up? Is it encrusted with dirt? Now remove your sock. Do you see a red spot on your foot? That's the start of a blister. Treat it immediately, and you'll be pain-free. Ignore it and you'll turn your walk into a sore-footed endurance test. What starts out as a minor discomfort can quickly become very serious. Be proactive about preventing blisters, and if you get one, be meticulous about taking care of it.

In most cases, blisters are caused by the simple rubbing of skin against the interior of a boot. If you're boot is too stiff and doesn't flex along with your foot as you walk, you can get a blister. This is probably the biggest reason why stiff leather boots have largely gone out of fashion for hikers. But ragged or dirty socks can also cause blisters. Ragged socks allow your skin to chafe directly against the boot's interior, and dirty socks wrinkle and fold, also rubbing against your feet instead of cushioning them.

To stay blister-free, the critical ingredients are clean feet, good socks, and good fitting boots. If there is any foot slippage from a compressed sock, accumulated dirt, or a too-small or too-stiff boot, you can rub up a blister in minutes.

The key to treating blisters is to work fast at the first sign of a hot spot. If you feel a hot spot coming on, never keep walking, assuming that the problem will go away. Stop immediately and remedy the situation. Cut a piece of moleskin to cover the offending spot, and secure the moleskin with white medical tape or even duct tape. Some people will skip the moleskin and just use duct tape on the hot spot; this works pretty well if the blister hasn't formed yet. We prefer a product called Spenco 2nd Skin, which helps to heal the blister as well as protect it. It will stick to your skin without tape. Ann Marie never hikes anywhere without a supply of Spenco 2nd Skin in her pack. She hasn't gotten a blister in more than a decade, but she has treated many friends' blisters with her handy Spenco stash, thus winning their eternal gratitude.

The key is to act fast. Don't wait an hour. Don't wait until you get back to camp. Take care of that blister (or the hot spot that precedes the blister) as soon as you feel it. If you don't, you could end up with an ugly situation like the one Scout Sorcic faced on a hiking trip in the red rock canyons of Utah.

Scout was trekking with a group of nine students and two instructors on a three-week National Outdoor Leadership School (NOLS) trip. The 143-mile course was designed to challenge the students with a variety of activities from rock climbing to off-trail navigation.

Scout wore her new lightweight hiking shoes. "Knowing I was going to be in the hot desert for three weeks, I bought shoes with mesh on the sides for ventilation, which seemed like a good idea at the time," Scout says. "I'd broken them in, walking in the shoes every day for about six months."

Scout's new shoes felt sturdy and comfortable, so she decided against bringing an extra pair on the trip. Her backpack was already loaded with a dromedary bag, eight days' worth of food, camping supplies, and canyoneering gear. Another pair of hiking shoes seemed like overkill.

Her group began their trek on a mesa, high above the desert canyons. "There were lots of cacti and lizards, but no trees," Scout says. "The sun was beating down on us." They plodded across the sandstone in the unrelenting heat. The temperature was so distracting, Scout failed to notice that sand was seeping into her shoes through the mesh sides, causing her feet to rub against the gritty fabric. When she reached camp that evening, her feet were inflamed. She peeled off her shoes and washed her swollen feet in cold water, then crawled into bed.

Unfortunately, when Scout woke in the morning, her raw, pink skin had erupted into puss-filled sores. "My feet get abused from hiking all the time, but they weren't used to the fine desert sand, the dehydration, and the heat," she says. "I had blisters the size of silver dollars on my heels."

Dehydration, heat, and overexertion made Scout's feet swell and rub even more against her sweaty, sand-filled shoes. "When I got back to camp, I pulled off my shoes and saw that my socks were red. It wasn't from the red sand. My blisters had popped," Scout recalls. Blood caked her heels and the blisters were now the size of golf balls.

But Scout shrugged off the pain. She was an avid backpacker and soccer player. Blistered feet were nothing new to her. "I figured they'd scab over and hurt for a couple of days, but then they'd be fine," Scout says.

But her blisters didn't get better. In the following days, she hobbled through the desert canyons, trying to ignore her painful feet. Halfway through the journey, she used a knife to cut the fabric off the backs of her hiking shoes. Having her heels exposed brought some relief, but with no protective barrier, dirt and sand filled her open wounds.

In the cool evenings at camp, Scout's instructors washed her sores in warm water, hoping they'd heal. "I would lie on my stomach while my instructors cleaned out my blisters. But every morning they would crack and bleed, making it a bit worse."

By this point, Scout's feet were in such terrible shape that she had become the weakest link in the group chain. Scout's instructors discussed evacuating her from the field. "My blisters were awful, and my morale was really low," she says.

But Scout's youthful determination prevailed, and she limped to the end of the 143-mile expedition.

"When I look back on my Utah trip, the only thing I remember is how badly my feet hurt," Scout says. "I had blisters on my feet for the entire twenty-one-day trek. They didn't fully heal till months later."

Now, Scout always packs an extra pair of shoes when she hikes, plus moleskin and several different weights of socks. She also has a quick fix she utilizes on the trail: if she feels a hotspot forming on her foot, she smooths a piece of duct tape over the problem area to protect the skin from friction.

"I really learned a lot on this hike," Scout says. "Feet are like your little backpacking psychiatrists. Happy feet make a happy trip."

Socks

We can't talk about hiking shoes without talking about socks. The two work in tandem to prevent blisters and other foot problems.

Your goal in choosing socks should be twofold. You want to prevent abrasion, and you want to move moisture away from your skin. Feet are sweaty things, unfortunately. Rule number one is do not wear all-cotton socks. Cotton absorbs sweat and dries very slowly. With cotton, your foot can get damp and mix with dirt, which can cause a hot spot to form on your foot. Instead, start with a sock made of a synthetic composite, such as wool and synthetic, or polypropylene, or CoolMax. These fabrics will at least partially wick moisture away from your skin.

Some hikers swear by wearing two pairs of socks, usually one thicker, cushioning pair over the top of a lightweight wicking liner sock. Others, like Ann Marie, swear by wearing only one pair of the lightest, thinnest socks available, so they fit like a second skin. Moisture-wicking is key. If you wear multiple socks, you may need to go up a full boot size to accommodate the extra layers around your feet.

On long trips of a week or more, you should have plenty of clean socks on hand, or plan on washing socks during your trip. As socks become worn, they also become compressed, dirty, and damp. If they fold over, you'll get a blister. If we have enough room in our packs, we'll carry fresh socks for every single day of our backpacking trip. It's a luxury, but it's worth it. We don't get blisters.

4
Gear That Matters

When you're planning a backpacking trip, the first gear you should consider are the Big Three: tent or sleeping shelter, sleeping system (sleeping bag and pad), and backpack. These are the three pieces of gear you really can't do without—or you can, but you won't be comfortable. They're the three items that pile the most weight on your back. They're also probably the three priciest equipment purchases that you'll make. If you choose them wisely, they'll serve you well for a decade or longer.

Sleeping Bag

There are enough sleeping bags on the market to make your head spin. Any gear-head or outdoors store salesperson can bore you with detailed pros and cons of every single bag they sell, so we'll leave that up to them. Instead, we'll distill down the main points to consider when buying a bag.

Rule number one: pay attention to the temperature rating. Back in 2009, most major American sleeping bag companies adopted the European Norm (EN) rating system. The ratings use a laboratory test to provide a range of temperatures based on gender and lower limit of survival. The idea is to indicate the lowest outdoor temperatures at which the bags will keep a man and a woman semi-warm, that is, not hypothermic. A separate indicator rates the bag for comfort, which is the temperature at which a man and a woman would sleep comfortably (women generally sleep colder than men). The rating system is based on the assumption that the sleeper is wearing long underwear and a hat, and his or her bag is lying on top of a one-inch-thick insulating pad. It also assumes that your bag is completely zipped, and your head and neck are cinched up in the hood.

The EN rating system is great for comparing one 15-degree bag to another 15-degree bag, but keep in mind that getting your body to an ideal temperature while sleeping outside isn't an exact science. If you put ten people in ten identical sleeping bags rated at 20 degrees, and they all sleep next to each other in the same 20-degree conditions, some people will be cold, some people will be hot, and some people will be just right. Your metabolism and your full (or empty) stomach have a huge impact on your body temperature.

Ann Marie often camps in the High Sierra above 10,000 feet, where summer nights are typically in the 30s, but she always uses a 0-degree bag. She knows from experience that if she slept in a bag rated for 30 degrees, she would be cold and cranky. Her experience is typical. Women often have trouble retaining body heat; so gals, consider buying a sleeping bag that is rated lower than your male companion's. Remember that if you get too warm, you can always unzip the thing, just like you throw off the blankets on your bed at home.

One way to correct for potential heat/cold variations is to pack along a lightweight sleep sack or sleeping bag liner. You put the sack or liner inside your bag if the night is cold (or just sleep in the sack or liner alone if the night is warm). Inserting a sleeping bag liner or sleep sack will raise the temperature rating of your sleeping bag by as much as 20 degrees.

One big advantage to using a liner inside your bag is that it is much easier to wash than a sleeping bag, especially a down sleeping bag. You can probably get through a whole summer of camping without having to wash your sleeping bag if your sweaty, dirty body touches only your liner or sleep sack. Of course, carrying a bag and a liner means you're carrying extra weight, and every ounce should be a carefully considered choice.

Down or Synthetic?

The other important decision in choosing a sleeping bag is whether you want it filled with down or synthetic fiber, or a combination of the two. Down is typically warmer and lighter, but if it gets wet, it's useless. A wet down sleeping bag will lose its loft and flatten out. (That's firsthand experience talking.) Most down bags today are water-resistant, but that's not the same as waterproof. If your water-resistant down bag gets caught in a downpour, it will be soaked and take a long time to dry.

Synthethic fibers are a very close second to down in terms of warmth and weight, and they dry a lot faster. They're also warmer when they are wet because they maintain their loft.

So which is the better choice—down or synthetic? It all boils down to preference, like whether you prefer a latte or a cappuccino. You can't go wrong with either one as long as you buy a quality, EN-rated bag. If you're an old-school backpacker, you probably worship at the altar of your down sleeping bag, which you've owned since Elvis was the King. But if you're just starting out and need to buy a new bag, a synthetic bag costs a lot less and will still keep you toasty.

Duck or goose down does have a certain cachet that inspires legions of devoted fans. Even veteran backpacker Jack Scheifly, who set his first down sleeping bag on fire fifty years ago, still reveres down bags.

At the time, Jack was a dedicated twelve-year-old Boy Scout who tromped around the Sierra Nevada every summer under the guidance of his ex-military Scoutmaster, Carl Fricke.

"This was the late 1960s, in the days of external frame packs and tube tents. Each of us kids made our own tube tent out of thick plastic sheeting that Mr. Fricke gave us. We kept the rain out of the tents with clothes pins. And we carried all this heavy stuff, even a cast-iron Dutch oven. Mr. Fricke always had to make pancakes," Jack says.

Jack's father had given him a down sleeping bag, which Jack proudly carried on many Boy Scout trips. But one night the Scouts didn't put up their tube tents, opting to sleep outside under the stars instead. Sometime around midnight, the rain came. It didn't last long, but by the time Jack managed to erect his tent and throw his sleeping bag inside, his down bag was soaked.

He shivered in that wet bag through the remaining hours of the night. "Even though I was in the bag, I was still cold. It was like sleeping in a wet noodle."

At the crack of dawn, Jack and the other rain-soaked Scouts got up and made a campfire.

"We got the fire going, and I managed to dry myself and my clothes and get warm. I took my down bag and hung it on a rope between two trees. It seemed like hours went by, and it still wasn't drying. It was totally soaked."

So young, resourceful Jack got the idea to move the bag closer to the fire, and you can guess what happened.

"Somehow a flame caught the bottom of my bag, and the down exploded," he recalls. "Nylon is scary. The bag ignited almost like it was spontaneous combustion."

Jack stomped on the bag to put the fire out. Then he examined what was left. "I lost a bunch of down from inside. But I still had to finish the trip, so I took some duct tape and taped up what was left of the bottom of my bag."

And fifty years later, Jack still worships at the altar of down.

Consider the Bag's Weight and Shape

If down versus synthetic doesn't make much difference, what does? Weight. What your sleeping bag weighs will have a huge impact on how heavy your pack is. But the lightest bag isn't necessarily the best bag because weight is often closely tied to a bag's shape and size. Mummy-shaped bags that are very narrow in the shoulder and hip will usually weigh less than bags that aren't as restrictive. But if you're someone who tosses and turns a lot at night, a super-skinny mummy bag can be uncomfortable. A wider bag might be a better choice, even though it weighs more. It all depends on how much a good night's sleep matters to you.

Some companies also make woman-specific bags that are shorter in length, wider at the hips, and narrower in the shoulders than men's bags. For women, these bags can save some weight while still providing enough room for comfort.

To sum up, keep in mind three factors when buying a new sleeping bag are: 1) temperature rating based on the EN scale; 2) down or synthetic filling (and there's no right or wrong here); and 3) size, shape, and weight of the bag. Oh yeah, there's also price—which is often the biggest deciding factor.

Terra's favorite bag is rated at 0 degrees, filled with a high-tech synthetic, and weighs 2.5 pounds. It's mummy-shaped, but not super narrow. She used to have a much more expensive bag that was lighter and narrower, but it made her feel like she was imprisoned in a straightjacket. When she's tucked inside her current bag, she sleeps like a baby.

Sleeping Pad

When you buy carpeting for your house, your friends and family will advise you that the quality of the carpet isn't nearly as important as the quality of the pad you put underneath it. It's the same with sleeping bags and sleeping pads. Of course you want to buy a quality bag that will keep you warm and cozy, but if you don't own a good pad to put underneath, you're wasting your money. Unless it's 85 degrees outside, most sleeping bags are practically useless without an insulating pad beneath them. The main selling point of a sleeping pad is to keep you warm, but coming in second is the idea that a good pad gets you off the bumpy ground, so you can sleep without pine cones and sticks pressing into your back.

Sleeping pads come in a dizzying array of weights, thicknesses, and even lengths. You can spend a little ($20) and get a basic foam pad with so much bulk that you need to strap it outside your pack.

It will insulate you from the ground and last until the next millennium, but offers little comfort. Or you can spend a lot ($100–$200) and get a top-of-the-line cushy air pad that is more than two inches thick and weighs only about one pound, give or take a few ounces.

The pad is one item you may want to consider splurging on. Go cheap on your pad and you may feel like you're sleeping on a rock.

Since sleep is such a personal matter, most backpackers have more difficulty choosing their sleeping pad than any other piece of equipment. What works for us won't necessarily work for you. Sometimes what works for us doesn't even work for us. Ann Marie owns four different backpacking pads plus a couple of extras for car camping, and she usually spends hours before a trip arguing with herself about which pad to pack.

Sleeping pads are given an R-value rating, which measures how well the pad will insulate your body from the ground. The higher the R-value, the warmer the pad will be. R-values of 2 to 3 are good for most conditions. R-values above 3 are good when the temperature drops to freezing or below, which it often does in summer nights in the high mountains. If you're planning to snow camp, you want an R-value of 5 or higher, and you may even want to pile up two pads and sleep on them.

Pads are available in various lengths, but unless you are determined to save every possible ounce, get a full-length pad that will accommodate your entire height plus a couple of extra inches. You don't want your feet coming off the pad all night long. Most pads are a standard twenty inches wide, but people with broad shoulders and those who tend to roll around a lot might want to splurge for a width of twenty-five or thirty inches.

Some air-filled foam pads are self-inflating, which means that you open up a valve located on one corner and the pad slowly fills itself with air. A group of aerospace engineers started the Therm-a-Rest company and pioneered the first self-inflating foam pads in the 1970s, and these pads still set the standard. Nonetheless, a common joke among backpackers is that "self-inflating" means "inflate it yourself." The pad does some of the work for you, but you still need to blow into the valve a few times.

A huge benefit to Therm-a-Rest foam pads is that they are filled with foam insulation inside their waterproof nylon shells. When you add air, you're doubly insulated with air and foam. That's some sweet cushioning. Get a self-inflating pad that is one or two inches thick, and it's almost like sleeping on your bed at home. (Okay, that may be an exaggeration.)

One nice feature of a self-inflating foam pad is that you can adjust its firmness by adding or subtracting a little air—even while you're lying on it. Therm-a-Rest also makes an ingenious chair kit that allows you to fold up your pad into a chair for sitting, and it weighs only about half a pound.

The third alternative to the cheap, closed-cell foam pad and the space-age self-inflating pad is the inflatable air pad. With these, you do all the inflating yourself, so call in a favor with your blow-hard friend. Some inflatable pads require fifteen or twenty solid lung blasts to fully inflate, which can be a bit of a chore after hiking all day. On the other hand, what else do you have to do? Since you can't check your email from camp, spend ten minutes getting red in the face while you blow up your air pad.

Inflatable air pads do not have foam insulation; they are filled with air only. The advantage is that they are extremely lightweight and pack down to a miniscule size, even if you get one that blows up to be three inches thick. Companies like Big Agnes and Exped are popular brands. Therm-a-Rest also makes an air-only inflatable pad. Make sure you compare these pads' R-values carefully since air alone is not the best insulator. The structure of the air pad also matters—if it doesn't have separate channels or baffles for its air compartments, it can feel like you're sleeping on a swimming pool float.

When Ann Marie tries to decide among her quiver of sleeping pads, she considers where she's going and how fast she wants to get there. As with most things in life, each of her pads comes with benefits and trade-offs. If she wants comfort most of all, she'll take her thickest Therm-a-Rest pad. But that means she's carrying extra weight, so it's not her choice for long-distance trips. If she wants to travel fast and doesn't plan to sleep on a bed of scree, she might

It takes some effort to blow up an inflatable air pad, but the payoff comes in a comfortable night's sleep.

take a thinner, lighter self-inflating pad, and sacrifice a little comfort. If she's going to the desert, she'll leave her super-spendy inflatable air pad at home. Instead, she'll pack her bulky-but-indestructible closed-cell foam pad. One clumsy step near a cactus and her air pad could be a pincushion.

One feature that we always look for in any kind of sleeping pad is a non-slippery, textured surface. There's nothing worse than waking up several times a night because you've slid off your pad, and now you're lying on the cold ground.

Although we are converts to both the self-inflating and inflatable air pads, each of us has experienced an unfortunate night when our pads sprung a leak. When an inflatable pad doesn't hold air, it doesn't insulate. If you can locate the miniscule pinhole that's causing the problem, you can patch it. Make sure that you always pack along the patch kit that is sold with these pads. But if you can't find that pinhole, or if the air leak is coming from a bad seam, not a pinhole, you're S.O.L.

The Ultralight Option

If you really hate to carry extra weight in your backpack, one of the best places to shave off pounds is with your sleeping system; that is, your bag and pad combined. Serious ultra-lighters will keep their bag-pad combo under three pounds. (Remember that Terra's bag alone weighs 2.5 pounds; her best inflatable pad weighs just under one pound.) To get your bag and pad under three pounds, you'll definitely need a high-end air pad. Ultralight backpackers often opt for three-quarter-length pads, both for less weight and less bulk in their packs. Plan on spending about $100 for a good ultralight pad. For a bag, you'll probably have to go with a down bag rated at 20 degrees or higher. Several companies make ultralight bags that weigh between one and two pounds, but be prepared for sticker shock. These retail for $400 and up, more than twice the price of a regular backpacking sleeping bag.

Pillows

Some more hardcore hiking friends will mock us for including "pillows" in a list of backpacking needs, but frankly, we love our pillows. Over the years, we have tried many options for supporting our heads while we sleep in the Great Outdoors, and none of them worked. We tried filling a stuff sack with extra clothes. We tried sleeping on the softest part of our backpacks. We even tried sleeping on our hydration system reservoirs.

Now we both carry our fancy-shmancy inflatable backpacking pillows. Terra prefers her Exped Air Pillow Ultralight and Ann Marie swears by her Sea to Summit Aeros Ultralight. Each weighs about two ounces and is worth more than ten times its weight in gold. The Exped has horizontal chambers that keep your head on the pillow, not rolling off on to the ground. The Sea to Summit has a unique cradle shape that does the same, plus a brushed surface that makes it cozy on your face. Both pillows cost about $45 and will help you to sleep deeply and happily. Two ounces of extra weight? Yeah. We'll shoulder that.

Tents

Just like with sleeping bags and pads, the myriad tent options are enough to make you tear your hair out and run screaming from your local outdoors store. But it doesn't have to be that hard. When buying a tent, consider three factors: seasonality, number of occupants, and weight. Do you want a tent you can use in the snow? Then you need a four-season tent. Otherwise, a three-season tent will do. Is the tent for you and your sweetie, or for you and your three Great Danes? With tents, size matters. If you try to put three people in a two-person tent, you're in for a long night.

Understand that not all two-person tents are the same size. Some are taller, some have more floor space, and so on. Compare all the dimensions to make sure you're getting what you want. The best way to figure out what you want is to visit an outdoors store that has a bunch of tents set up on the showroom floor. Sit and lay down inside each tent and notice the differences. It won't take long to figure out what feels best. Need more head room? Extra floor space? Taller walls? Most tents are tall enough so that you can sit up or kneel in them, but some people feel claustrophobic if the tent ceiling is too near their face when they lie down. Experiment with the tents on display and see what feels good to you.

On longer trips, it's nice to have a slightly bigger tent. That way you don't feel claustrophobic when you need to spend a rainy afternoon inside, and there's plenty of room to store your pack inside out of the rain. If you're just going out for a couple of nights, you can probably make do with a smaller, lighter tent. Ann Marie has a one-person tent for when she hikes solo (it's a squeeze, but her eighty-pound dog can fit inside, too), and a larger tent for sharing with a friend (or to let her dog really stretch out).

We've also learned that if more than one person is in the tent, it's nice to have two doors. That way your partner doesn't have to crawl over the top of you when he or she goes outside to pee at 2 a.m.

Then there's the whole issue of weight. Are you comfortable carrying a 3.5-pound tent, or would you rather shave that weight to two pounds? Tents are one of the "Big Three," that is, the gear that weighs the most, along with sleeping systems and backpacks. To save weight, sacrifice a little tent size and also some features. The more doors and zippers and mesh panels and fancy doo-dads a tent has, the more it's going to weigh.

If you're traveling solo and trying to save weight, you could opt for a tunnel-shaped tent that isn't freestanding and doesn't give you as much height. "Tube tents," as they were called in the 1960s and 1970s, were the backpackers' tent choice for many years. These tents are basically a glorified tarp that weighs a pound or less. The triangular-shaped tube has no frame and no stakes and is held up by a rope strung between two trees. It's rare to find a tube tent that fits more than one person.

With the popularity of the ultralight or fast-packing movement, everything old is new again, and tube tents are popular once more. If you're the kind of person who cuts off your toothbrush handle to save half an ounce—yeah, that's a bit extreme—you might like camping in a tube tent. Some ultralight backpackers go even lighter and carry just a tarp, which they can use as a ground-cloth below their sleeping pad, or fashion into a tube tent if wet weather threatens.

When clouds start building, a sturdy, waterproof tent and rain fly are worth the extra weight.

Adam Peters wouldn't recommend it, though. Adam, a super-fit hiker and gonzo backpacker in his sixties, has spent many decades roaming around the Sierra. He says that much of his outdoor knowledge came from trial and error, like figuring out that a good tent was worth its weight, even though it cost him an extra pound or two.

Adam says he was an ultralight hiker back in the 1970s, long before it was cool. "I've always hated heavy backpacks," he says. "I'm kind of a small guy and I like to hike off-trail and up peaks and over rocks."

Adam especially hated carrying a tent. "I got away for years with carrying a tube tent that weighed less than a pound," he says. Modern versions of tube tents have flaps that close, but Adam's tube tent was open on the ends.

"In 1978, I was camping with some buddies up at Bishop Lake," he recalls. He and a friend each had a tube tent; two other friends shared a "real" tent.

"While we were up there, Tropical Storm Norman hit California—unbeknownst to us. All we knew was that it started to rain like hell. So of course I put up my tube tent."

The tropical cyclone Norman was actually rated as a hurricane, and it caused flash flooding in many areas of the state. In a two-day period, five to seven inches of rain dumped on the Sierra's lower elevations. In the higher mountains, a blizzard killed four people, and at least seventeen hikers went missing.

"During the night, I got soaked. My buddy in the other tube tent got soaked, too. When the morning came, we went over to our friends' tent and said, 'You have to let us in. We're cold.' The four of us just sat there in that tent in the pouring rain for three hours. There wasn't a lot of room."

The rain didn't show any signs of letting up. "Finally, my buddy and I decided it was best just to get out of there. We couldn't stay with those guys and our tents were no good, so we hiked out," he says.

It was only four miles back to the trailhead, but the rain was biblical in force. Adam and his friend practically ran down the trail. When they reached the car, Adam's friend turned on the heater for warmth. "At one point, the car was so hot inside that my friend was sweating. But I couldn't stop shivering," he says.

Eventually his body heat returned, but this was as close as Adam has ever come to experiencing hypothermia.

"The thing that saved us on that trip was our friends having the good tent. If we hadn't been hiking with them, I'm sure we would have gone faster and hiked in farther. I might not have gotten out at all."

So Adam learned from the experience and went out and bought a real tent. "I wasn't happy about having to carry it because it weighed about three pounds. But it was waterproof," he says. "Tube tents will help you in a drizzle, but they're not effective in real rain."

Okay, now fast-forward about twenty years for Part Two of Adam's tent lessons.

"I went backpacking with my thirteen-year-old son. He wasn't that wild about backpacking, but he did it because I wanted to go,"

Adam says. "I had the same single-walled tent that I'd bought twenty years ago, which had held up great up to that point.

"We had a big, rainy night, and my tent was so old that it was no longer waterproof. The water soaked into the seams in the ceiling and the floor. It made a little lake inside the tent that was about a half-inch deep. My son was sleeping on a Therm-a-Rest, which kept him out of the lake and pretty dry. I had a Therm-a-Rest, too, but I also had a down sleeping bag, which got completely soggy. I put on all my clothes and tried to stay warm. I was shivering. Meanwhile my son was saying stuff like, 'Backpacking is stupid. Why are we doing this, Dad?'"

Adam and his son made it through the uncomfortable night, and luckily the rain stopped by morning.

"I knew that the lesson here was not just to have a good tent, but also to make sure that it's still waterproof. After that experience, I started to check my tent for waterproofing before I'd go anywhere with it. Every summer, I'd get my tent out, set it up in the yard, and run a hose over it," he says.

Then came Part Three of Adam's tent lessons.

"I was backpacking up in Pioneer Basin. This time I had another tent that was only about ten years old. I was too cheap to buy a new one, but I'd tested the tent with the hose, so I thought it was okay. We had a rainstorm one night, and it got really windy—not gale force but enough to stress the tent. I was laying inside, and suddenly the seams split wide open. The glue that held the seams gave way, and the top of my tent opened up to the rain.

"But this time I knew what to do: I put my sleeping bag away quickly so it would stay dry, and I put on all my clothes and my rain gear. I had some safety pins and some tape, and I tried to seal up the tent, but it didn't work. So I just lay on the floor tucked away in a corner where the seams were still holding. This time I managed to say pretty dry, but I had to sleep in my rain gear," he says.

We asked Adam to summarize his School of Hard Knocks tent lessons, and he gave us three rules to live by: 1) Don't trust a tube tent in heavy rain. Instead, get a freestanding tent that can stand up to the

The footprint on most one- and two-person tents is small enough that you can set them up even in tight spaces.

weather. 2) Set up your tent in the backyard every year. Run a hose on it to make sure it's still waterproof. 3) While you're running the hose, shake your tent around. Test the seams. Make sure it's solid.

"Because when you need a tent, you really need it," Adam says.

Staking the Tent

Another advantage of a "real" tent versus a tube tent is that a real tent can be staked. Most tents are freestanding, meaning they are held up by two or three curved aluminum poles that give the tent structural integrity. Freestanding frames make tents fairly sturdy, and they can be staked at several points for additional support in high winds. If your tent has stakes, always use them, even if there isn't a wisp of wind. Terra was careless about staking her tent on balmy days until her friend Kerri Stevenson told her about a near-disaster camping trip in Utah's Canyonlands National Park.

Kerri and her husband, Derek De Oliveira, headed to Canyon-lands to hike and mountain bike in September 2015. On their first night, the couple car-camped a short distance from the White Rim trailhead at Shafer Campground, where a high, sprawling mesa over-looked etched buttes and red rock canyons. But when they set up their tent, the hard ground wouldn't accommodate their tent stakes. There was nothing but solid rock.

Scattered around the campsite were piles of large, loose rocks. The couple guessed that other campers had used the rocks as make-shift tent stakes because some of them were stacked in perfect, tent-shaped rectangles. Kerri and Derek decided to try the same method.

"I figured all we had to do was pile the rocks up on all of the tent points," Kerri remembers.

By the time the couple piled the rocks and threw their camp pads and sleeping bags inside the tent, it was night. They were cook-ing dinner when out of nowhere, gusts of wind and torrential rain assaulted them.

"The entire sky filled with lightning and the wind picked up," Kerri says. "We jumped in our truck to wait out the storm because we knew it would be better than being on the rocks."

The thundering squall pelted the campground and the truck, which was parked about thirty yards away. At one point, Kerri leapt out of the vehicle and bolted through the downpour to see how her tent was holding up. She checked the stability of the rocks, and in a last-ditch effort, heaved a small boulder into the shelter to weigh it down.

"I threw a huge-ass rock inside. It probably weighed twenty-five pounds," she says. "I was just trying to keep the tent there. The storm came in so fast, I didn't have time to figure out anything else."

Then she dashed back to the truck. In another thirty minutes, the storm passed, and the night was dark and calm. The pair grabbed their headlamps and ventured out to investigate their campsite.

"It was the funniest moment," Kerri said. "We went around the corner and realized our tent was gone. It wasn't anywhere in sight. All that was left was a little circle of rocks."

They walked around the camp perimeter, peering through the darkness for their missing shelter while trying not to fall off the mesa's edge, a sheer cliff that plummeted to the canyon floor.

"All of a sudden, we saw our tent hanging from the cliff," Kerri relays. "It was caught on a branch, and it still had this big, stupid rock in it."

Kerri and Derek stretched out over the precipice, grappling to reach the trapped tent. They managed to retrieve it, but the tent and sleeping pads were shredded. "The wind had tumbled the tent through cacti and brambles, and the rock had popped our Therm-a-Rests and ripped our rain fly."

Fortunately, the couple was able to salvage their gear. "I had packed smart and brought a Therm-a-Rest patch kit. We were able to patch them up," she recalls. She had also packed duct tape and tweezers. "I duct-taped the heck out of our rain fly, and used the tweezers to pick all the thorns and spikes from our tent."

It doesn't matter how balmy the weather is when you put up your tent. Storms can come in on a moment's notice, and in a competition between your tent and the wind, your tent will always lose.

To stake your tent properly, start at the four corners. Drive in the stakes at a 45-degree angle (this makes it easier if the ground is very hard). To apply more force, find a small rock to use as a hammer. Just don't overdo it, or you'll risk breaking your stakes. Once the four tent corners are staked out, attach stakes to all the other points until the body and floor of the tent are taut.

If you choose to camp on solid rock like the granite slabs that are common throughout many mountain ranges, you will have to get creative. Wrap a line from your tent around the middle of a stake, knot it tight, and place the stake on the ground sideways. Then place at least two rocks on the stake, one on either side of the line, to weigh it down. Sticks or hiking poles can also work if your stakes are too short. This is known as a "deadman anchor." Some people will just wrap their tent lines around heavy rocks, but as Kerri will tell you, that's not a bombproof solution in high winds.

Camping on solid granite requires creative tent staking.

The Backpack

We've spent a lot of time talking about the big stuff you need to carry on a backpacking trip. But that begs the question: What am I going to put all that stuff in? Grandpa's old Army duffel bag might

98

work, but you'll be happier with a high-quality backpack, one that's carefully fitted to your body and the load you're carrying.

It used to be that a backpacker's first decision was to choose between an internal and external frame pack, but the latter have largely gone the way of the cigarette-smoking brontosaurus. If you were in the Boy Scouts or Girl Scouts in the 1970s or 1980s, you probably owned an external frame pack. Those big, bulky packs had their merits—particularly the way they kept the load farther away from the body, which allowed for good air movement. But they also created serious balance problems, especially if they weren't loaded perfectly.

Most packs sold today have internal frames, which are narrow and form-fitting. They are designed for stability and ideal for activities that require a lot of movement, like climbing, skiing, or backpacking. Internal frame backpacks usually come with lots of bells and whistles, such as a built-in suspension system designed to keep the weight

A smartly packed backpack can mean the difference between a fun trip and a tough endurance test.

from touching your body, a hydration bladder, a sleeping bag compartment, various attachment points for clipping on equipment like snowshoes or hiking poles, and an elaborate system of outside pockets where you can stash away Snickers bars like a chipmunk stashes away nuts. Depending on the size and features of the pack, it will probably weigh somewhere around three to five pounds.

The only other type of pack to consider is an ultralight pack, which doesn't have any supporting frame at all. If you plan to hike all 2,650 miles of the Pacific Crest Trail, you'll probably want an ultralight frameless pack, which is basically a high-tech, souped-up version of Grandpa's old Army duffel. With a frameless pack, you get a lightweight sack with very few frills, so you eliminate a great deal of weight. Many frameless packs weigh as little as a pound, which is awesome. But you also sacrifice some comfort.

How much your backpack weighs when empty matters a lot. But what matters even more is comfort and fit. Put thirty pounds in an uncomfortable or ill-fitting backpack and it feels like fifty pounds. Trust us on this.

Your empty backpack holds a considerable proportion of the total weight you'll be carrying, so it's important to carefully consider the weight issue. As ultralight gear has improved over the years, we've converted to a midpoint philosophy. The two of us own many packs, but the ones we reach for most are our "mid-weight, ultralight" packs. That sounds like a jumbo-shrimp-style oxymoron, but actually it's a happy medium. Right now we're both carrying Osprey ultralight packs that weigh about 2.5 pounds. They're not as featherlight as many ultralight packs, but they allow us many of the comfort features we like in our more traditional packs.

Once you've decided between traditional versus ultralight—or chosen something in the middle, like we have—there's still a lot of comparing to do. You could just get started by trying on every backpack in your local outdoors store, or narrow down the field by deciding what's most important to you.

Start with capacity; that is, how much junk will it hold. You need a PhD in math to understand how pack volume is calculated.

Keep it simple and follow these guidelines: If you know you'll never backpack for more than two nights, get a smaller-capacity pack, something along the lines of thirty to fifty liters. If you plan to go on three- to five-day trips, look at packs in the fifty- to seventy-liter range. These are what salespeople call the "Weekend Warrior Pack," and they're generally the most popular packs on the market, so that means the widest range of choices and prices. If you own a lot of ultralight gear, like your sleeping bag, pad, tent, and so on, you can get away with something smaller, maybe forty to fifty liters, but if you have regular-weight equipment, you'll need fifty to seventy liters.

For week-long or longer trips, or if you're the troop leader for a pack of Girl Scouts or a parent carrying two kids' stuff, you'll need a gonzo pack, something like seventy to ninety liters.

A few words of caution are in order here. It might be easy to assume that when buying a backpack, bigger is better. Wrong, wrong, wrong. A bigger backpack only encourages you to bring more stuff, and bringing more stuff is heavy. You will complain a lot more and hike a lot slower. A smaller-sized backpack will force you to leave stuff out of the pack that probably should be left out, like that Oxford English Dictionary you can never part with.

And here's another lesson from two people who have done this the wrong way: If you're hiking with another person or a group, you don't want to have the largest pack in the group. Otherwise everybody will say stuff like, "Hey, Terra has that huge pack—she can carry out the trash!" Or worse: "Ann Marie can carry this cast-iron frying pan."

Okay, so now you've considered capacity. The next issue is sizing. Backpacks come in four sizes (extra small, small, medium, and large) that correspond to a human's torso length. As you'd expect, with various manufacturers out there, there is a lot of discrepancy between what these sizes entail. A medium in an Osprey pack is not necessarily the same as a medium in a Gregory pack. You can have a friend measure your torso size for you, or an outdoors store salesperson can do it. You lay a tape measure along your back from the "shelf" at the top of your hip bones to the bony bump at the base of your neck. (For all of you in medical school, that's your seventh cervical verte-bra.) That's your torso length. A pack with the right torso length will sit comfortably on your hips, which is where you want the weight to be.

That brings us to another point: make sure the hip belt is well padded, so you don't get sore spots on your hips or lower back. Another key feature to look for in a pack is good ventilation. We're fans of packs that have a suspended mesh panel that eliminates the "sweaty back syndrome" we used to suffer with. With the mesh panel, the pack actually sits a couple of inches away from your back, allowing air to flow through.

Lots of pockets matter, too. It's great to be able to put a few trail snacks and your camera or smart phone in an outside pocket, so you don't have to dig through your pack to find them.

And finally, we prefer packs that have removable top lids, so we can take them off and use them for day-hiking during layover days on multi-day backpack trips. Usually the pack lid converts into a fanny-pack or waist-pack, and it's just the right size for carrying a bottle of water and a few emergency items.

The backpacks are packed and ready, and it's time for adventure.

Women-Specific Packs

As women backpackers, we highly recommend that women buy woman-specific backpacks. For decades, Ann Marie tromped around the wilderness with a men's backpack. She had many fabulous adventures with this pack and never yearned for anything better. Then one fine day, that pack met its end. It had been held together with only duct tape and wishful thinking for some time, and Ann Marie grew tired of hikers pointing and snickering as she passed them on the trail.

The moment Ann Marie tried on a woman-specific pack, all her womanly curves cried a joyful and resounding "YES!" and she plunked down $300 on the spot. Women's packs are narrower than men's packs. The shoulder straps are closer together, and the hip belts are canted to fit a woman's hips. And this isn't a case of manufacturer's pink-washing, because these packs don't come in insipid girlie colors. They're serious packs that are sized for a woman's body.

Clothing

Terra is much more fashionable than Ann Marie, but neither is going to try to tell you exactly what you should wear for hiking. We will tell you that less is more when it comes to backcountry accouterment— you're probably going to wear the same T-shirt for three days straight, so don't bother packing three T-shirts.

Keep this in mind: When you're backpacking, you get dirty. You slather on sunscreen and bug spray and you sit around in the dirt. If you're lucky, you can jump in a lake to clean off some grime, but that's only if the weather cooperates and the lake water is warm enough. After a couple of days in the backcountry, you're going to be a bit . . . well, unclean. So accept that and move on.

You might think it would be smart to bring lots of changes of clothes so you'll have clean stuff to wear, but remember that you'll just be putting those clean clothes on top of your dirty body. That's like putting lipstick on a pig. No offense.

Below is an outline for a clothes packing list for a four-night back-packing trip. If it seems too minimalist, keep in mind that this is the clothing you are carrying, which is in addition to the clothing you are already wearing. If you go out for fewer than four nights, don't change the quantities of anything except socks.

Here's our list:

1. **One T-shirt.** Make sure it is some kind of wicking material like polyester, nylon, or a quick-drying synthetic, not cotton. Cotton gets damp and stays damp; it doesn't wick moisture away from your skin.
2. **One long-sleeved shirt.** This is useful in case the mosquitoes are bad, or you need to cover up from the sun. Any lightweight, quick-drying material is fine except cotton.

Even in mid-summer, hikers in the high mountains may need gloves and a wool hat. Don't leave home without them.

3. **One pair of lightweight, quick-drying hiking pants with legs that zip off.** You can wear them as shorts or pants.

4. **One very warm jacket.** A down-filled or synthetic fiber-filled jacket is perfect because it weighs nothing and squishes into a tiny space. Ann Marie never goes anywhere without her lightweight purple puffy. If you're hiking somewhere it might rain, keep in mind that synthetics dry faster than down when wet. If you insist on down, make sure you have a rain poncho or jacket that you can wear over your down jacket to keep it dry.

5. **Something clean to sleep in.** Terra likes a pair of lightweight polypropylene long underwear. She can also wear this as a base layer under her clothing if it is cold in the daytime.

6. **Underwear (including sports bras).** Purists will insist on one fresh pair of undies per day, but if you're bringing that many, for heaven's sake make sure they are nylon or polyester and weigh next to nothing. One good sports bra can last for two or three days, just like a T-shirt can.

7. **Three pairs of socks, or one pair for every day you'll be hiking.** While there was some ranting about the importance of socks in the previous chapter, please indulge us in a bit more ranting. Socks are the one clothing item you should never scrimp on. Ann Marie wears very thin ankle-height socks that weigh almost nothing, so she brings a clean pair for each day of her trip. Changing socks every day is one of the smartest ways to keep your feet happy. Extra socks can also serve you well in an emergency. You can wear them on your feet or even your hands.

8. **Wool hat and gloves if you're headed for the mountains (yes, it can snow in July in the Rockies or the Sierra Nevada).** If it's cold at night, wear your wool hat to bed and your entire body will feel warmer.

9. **Sun hat.** A hat with a big brim that will keep your mug out of the sun. Technically this shouldn't be on this list because you'll be wearing it, not carrying it. But it's so important that we put it on the list anyway.

Protect your face, ears, and neck from the sun with a wide-brimmed hat.

10. **Rain gear.** After carefully consulting the weather forecast, Ann Marie will sometimes go without rain gear, claiming that if it rains, she will put up her tent and wait it out. But she always carries a $3, ultra-thin plastic emergency rain poncho. These ponchos weigh only a few ounces and are large enough to cover her and her pack, so technically she's still carrying rain gear. If you're headed to a notoriously wet place like Olympic National Park in Washington, bring serious rain gear. The extra weight is worth it.

11. **A pair of lightweight sandals or camp shoes.** Yup, these are a luxury item, but if you've hiked fifteen miles in your boots today, it's nice to have a pair of flip flops or Crocs to wear in camp tonight. Ann Marie has had the same pair of TEVAs for twenty years. They weigh only a few ounces and let her feet breathe after a long day on the trail. They're also good for crossing streams if she doesn't want to get her boots wet.

Everything should fit inside a stuff sack, and it should weigh no more than five pounds. If your clothes-filled stuff sack weighs more, get rid of some stuff. Seriously. You'll be thankful later when you're hiking up Heart Attack Pass.

If your stuff sack isn't waterproof, it's smart to put your clothes in a plastic bag inside the stuff sack. That way if it rains or if your pack falls in the creek, your clothes stay dry.

The Joys of Layering

Chapter 7: Weather and Elements includes a discussion on how hypothermia is one of the biggest killers in the outdoors. Carrying a good tent, sleeping bag, and pad will go a long way toward preventing hypothermia, but, more critically, your clothing is your first line of defense against wet, cold, and wind.

When you pack for your backpacking trip, imagine that it gets really cold and you need to put on everything you have. You should have several different layers (T-shirt, long-sleeved shirt, jacket, etc.) that fit on top of one another. The layer that's closest to your skin should always be a wicking layer—polyester or nylon, or some other kind of synthetic fiber that is breathable and dries quickly. Cotton does not fit that bill. The old saying "cotton kills" is unfortunately true. Cotton gets wet and stays wet. So does wool. You don't want wet clothing next to your skin; it's a recipe for hypothermia. Ladies, your sports bra should be wicking and quick-drying, too.

Color Your World

When you pick out your outer-layer hiking clothes, don't be a wall-flower. Buy the brightest, most garish colors you can find, especially for larger pieces like puffy jackets or rain gear. Your goal is to stand out, not blend in. If you're ever in a situation where you need to be found—whether by your hiking partner who has wandered away from camp or by search-and-rescue professionals—bright colors can make all the difference. The more stuff you have in your pack that

In the backcountry, layering is key to dressing for success. Make sure your outer layers don't blend in with your surroundings.

is hot magenta, bright red, or school-bus yellow, the more chance a helicopter can spot you.

For base layers, (T-shirts, etc.) basic black has its place, but not on a hot sunny day. Light-colored or white base layers will keep you cooler. Black is great for winter days when you're trying to absorb heat.

A Few Words about Washing

If you intend to wash your clothes in the wilderness, fine. But don't use soap. Never. Not even that stuff that advertisers market as biodegradable soap. There's no such thing. Some tiny amphibian or insect is going to swallow that nasty stuff, and it might kill them.

And while you're going without soap, consider washing your underwear (or socks, or whatever) in a large pot by your campsite, then dumping the dirty water at least 300 feet from a lake or stream. Why? Because your clothes contain residual soap from the last time you washed them at home, and you don't want that soap polluting Pristine Creek. There is nothing more discouraging than hiking ten miles to a beautiful mountain lake only to find soap bubbles floating on the surface.

Ditto for your body and your hair. Your skin is covered with three days' worth of sunscreen and mosquito repellent. No fish wants to drink that stuff. Wash yourself with a big pot of water far away from any water source, and don't use soap.

If you're one of those people who ranks cleanliness right up there with godliness, consider hauling in a lightweight solar shower. These plastic wonders consist of a sturdy bag with a small tube and nozzle at the bottom. You fill them with lake water in the morning, hang them up on a tree branch in the sun, and by four in the afternoon you have a warm shower. Yes, this is a one-pound luxury item, but for some, it might be worth it. Clean freaks, rejoice.

Stoves and Cooking Needs

Some backpackers are mentally tough. They set out on the trail with only a jar of peanut butter, a bag of almonds, and a bunch of trail bars. They eat only to fuel their bodies. They don't think about food every minute of the day.

Not us. We like a cup of tea around midday, preferably with some cookies. We like a backcountry latte or mocha first thing in the morning. And we like a hot dinner at night. In short, we like our camping stove, and we wouldn't think of going backpacking without a stove for cooking hot food and drinks.

There are a few categories in camp stoves, the most common being white gas/variable fuel stoves, isobutane-propane (isopro) blend stoves, and integrated systems like the Jetboil line of stoves or the MSR Reactor stove. Each has its merits. But for those of you whose eyes glaze over when you detect gear jargon coming your way, let's skip right to the bottom line: Ninety-nine percent of the time, you can have anything you want to eat in the backcountry just by boiling water. And if all you need to do is boil water, then skip all the stove decision-making and buy yourself an integrated stove-and-pot system, like the Jetboil or MSR Reactor. The stove and pot join together and work in tandem to boil water fast and efficiently.

An integrated stove system makes camp cooking fast and efficient.

We're Jetboil fans because we love the simplicity of carrying one stove and one pot that does everything we need. We have been carrying these integrated stoves since they first went on the market, and we've cooked up some yummy backcountry meals. Even mountain trout can be cooked in boiling water, but if you're planning to catch and eat a lot of them, you might want the luxury of frying them. In that case, you can always buy the Jetboil frying pan attachment. This will run you about $50 extra, but allows you to fry fish or flip pancakes.

With an integrated cooking system, you can eat right out of the pot you cooked in by just unscrewing it from the stove base. To be more civilized, bring along another plate or bowl or cup. You also need some sort of utensil; we're fond of the all-purpose spork. And of course, you need to bring a canister of gas because the stove won't boil water without it.

Water Filter

You should never go backpacking without a device for filtering natural water sources, unless you plan to spend a lot of time boiling water—and waiting for it to cool so you can drink it. Plan on adding about a half-pound of weight to your pack for a pump-style water filter or UV filter. Read Chapter 5: Water and Food, for a discussion on the various water treatment options.

Kits for First Aid, Hygiene, Emergencies, Repairs

Let's face it. If your body needs serious first aid, or if your gear needs serious repairs, your trip is probably going to end a little sooner than you planned. But in the case of minor first-aid issues or minor gear repairs, it's great to have some supplies at the ready.

For first-aid, hygiene, and personal care:

1. Bandages, band aids, gauze bandage
2. Spenco 2nd Skin or moleskin for treating blisters
3. Triple antibiotic ointment for cuts or scrapes

A few basic first aid items in a Ziploc bag can keep the "minor" in "minor emergency."

4. Advil or Aleve for headaches, minor aches, and pains
5. Any required medications for your group (Is anyone allergic to bee stings?)
6. Mosquito repellent
7. Lightweight trowel for burying human waste (poop)
8. Toothbrush and toothpaste
9. Hand sanitizer
10. Sunscreen, lip balm, sunglasses
11. Packet of baby wipes
12. Oral antihistamine like Benadryl
13. Local anesthetic like Benzocaine

For on-the-trail repairs:

1. Forty-foot length of parachute cord (can work as a dog leash or be used to hang food away from critters)
2. Duct tape

3. Safety pins, especially a few large ones
4. Super glue

The last element you need to cram into your pack is perhaps the most important: your Emergency Kit, which is a variation on the Day-Hikers Checklist discussed in detail in Chapter 2: Wilderness Smarts. You never want to go out in the wilderness without a few basic items that can save your life, or at least make it a lot more comfortable. These include:

1. Headlamp plus extra batteries, or a couple of tiny "squeeze" flashlights for backup
2. Whistle
3. Fire-starting supplies
4. Detailed topographic maps for the area you're hiking in
5. Compass
6. Cell phone (put it in "airplane mode" to save the battery; this works as a way to tell time if you don't wear a watch)
7. Personal locator beacon (see Chapter 1: Risk and Rescue)
8. Mylar blanket (for emergency shelter or treating someone with hypothermia, can also be used for signaling a helicopter)
9. Swiss Army knife

Other Useful Stuff to Put in Your Pack

Lisa Whatford, a thirty-five-year search-and-rescue veteran professional who finds missing people in three different California mountain counties, has figured out a few things about what to put in your pack and what not to. Her motto: "If you have what you need, and if you are not hot or cold or hungry or thirsty, you can have a fabulous time on any adventure." To that end, she's a huge fan of items that can serve multiple purposes. Here are a few of her favorite double-duty items:

1. **A bandana** absorbs sweat and keeps your head warm, serves as a headband, beanie, or neck covering. You can wet it and wrap

it around your head or neck on a hot day. It can also be used for first aid or as a strap, or even to hang a bell or something else around your dog's neck.

2. **Plastic Ziploc bags** are waterproof and see-through. They can be used to organize and segregate stuff in your pack, so you're not always digging around for your reading glasses or a pen. Ziplocs are also perfect for packing out trash. You'll need a few in every size, from super small for your matches and lighter to extra-large for clothes. If your pack gets wet, everything packed inside a plastic Ziploc stays dry. Her words of wisdom: "I pack my sleeping bag in a trash bag always. A wet sleeping bag is useless. The same is true for a wet puffy jacket."

3. **A large black garbage bag,** the kind you fill with leaves or pine needles from your yard. Garbage bags fit over backpacks nicely and keep them dry when it rains. Garbage bags with a few holes cut in them also fit over *you* nicely, and keep you dry (or at least partially dry) when it rains. On long trips, garbage bags can be used to keep your smelly, dirty clothes separate from your clean clothes in your pack. Buy the heavy-duty kind and they'll last for several trips.

How Much Weight Can You Carry?

There's a formula for this. We like the formula. We also like varying from the formula. We'll spell out the formula with appropriate mathematical gravitas; you figure out the variations. Here it is:

Your body weight × 25 percent = How much weight you should carry

Some people increase this percentage to 30 percent or even 32 percent and feel just fine. A lot has to do with how much lean muscle mass you carry. In other words, a man who is six feet tall and weighs 180 pounds can probably carry more than a man who is five feet, six inches tall and weighs the same, since Tall Guy is likely leaner and meaner.

On the other hand, some people decrease this percentage to 20 percent or even less, but then they're forced to purchase ultralight gear, especially the Big Three: tent, backpacking, and sleeping system (bag and pad).

Terra is a petite five foot, three inches and weighs 110 pounds. She carries a maximum of 27.5 pounds when she backpacks. Ann Marie is taller and stronger. She's five feet, seven inches and weighs 130 pounds, so at the 25 percent calculation, she could carry 32.5 pounds. But she likes to hike fast and being weighed down makes her cranky, so she rarely carries more than thirty pounds. You might not believe that 2.5 pounds would make a difference, but it does, especially when you're pounding your way up Merciless Mountain.

Budgeting the Weight

As an example, here's how we might budget the weight we'll carry for a four-night trip. Ann Marie is comfortable carrying a bit less than 25 percent of her body weight, or about thirty pounds. Here's how she splits it up:

- Stuff sack full of clothing, including rain gear, parka, and camp sandals = five pounds
- Sleeping bag (and liner and pillow if you want them) = three pounds
- Sleeping pad = one pound
- Tent with rain fly, poles, and stakes = three pounds
- Cooking gear, water purification, and food = nine pounds (plan on 1.5 pounds of food per day per person, so for four nights, one person carries six pounds of food plus three pounds of cooking and water filtering gear, including gas for the camp stove, a pot, a cup, utensils)
- Bear canister to store food and scented items = three pounds (only necessary if traveling in bear country or where required by law; see Chapter 6: Dealing With Critters)
- Backpack (when empty) = 2.5 pounds

- Emergency gear and toiletries (first-aid kit, medications, tooth-brush, headlamp, trowel, matches, whistle, trail maps, personal locator beacon, cell phone, etc.) = 1.5 pounds

That makes twenty-eight pounds, so that leaves two freebie pounds for "fun stuff" like a camping chair or chair kit, playing cards, camera, books, fishing rod, sketch pad, harmonica, etc. Note that the pack weight drops to twenty-five pounds if you don't need to carry a bear canister, so that leaves five extra freebie pounds. Pack up the *World Book Encyclopedia*!

Now, if Ann Marie doesn't hike solo, she can share her tent, cooking gear, bear canister, and water purification device with her hiking partner. If they split up that stuff, she gets to carry more "fun stuff," which in her case is usually books. And chocolate. This is by far one of the greatest advantages of hiking in a group of two or more—if you're close friends, you can share the weight of the cooking gear, the first-aid kit, the tent(s), the water filtering device, etc.

We don't count hiking boots, sun hat, sunglasses, or trekking poles in the weight count because those will be on our bodies or in our hands. We add up only what goes in the pack.

And here's a funny thing we figured out after many years of not figuring it out. Whether we're heading out for two nights or five, the amount of weight we need only changes by a couple of pounds—extra food and extra socks. Everything else is the same. The weight budget shown above will cover Ann Marie for four nights, but she'd save only three pounds by backpacking for two nights instead of four. When this "aha moment" finally hit us, we decided to take a few extra days off work and extend our vacation.

Double-Check Your Gear, and Stay Humble

Let's end this long chapter on backpacking and hiking gear with one of our favorite stories from one of our favorite outdoorsy friends. Even if you forget everything else you've read, you'll probably remember Harriot's story, and the lessons she learned could serve us all.

As a travel writer who specializes in California and former editor for *Backpacker*, Harriot Manley considered herself well prepared for a backpack trip to Mount Whitney, which, at 14,505 feet, is the highest, most formidable peak in the lower forty-eight states. She and her friend Catherine, both mothers in their forties, decided to make the trip in September 2002. They were looking forward to a little vacation away from their kids.

"Neither of us had been to Mt. Whitney," Harriot says. "But we were both experienced backpackers and pretty comfortable going on a little mini-escape."

They knew the hike was long and arduous, but the two friends had been training. They owned all the latest backpacking equipment, and before they left, they made sure to check everything. They laid out their supplies, packed their backpacks, and checked that their weight was carefully balanced. Then they packed everything in the car and headed to the town of Lone Pine, where they spent two days acclimating to the high elevation they'd be facing on Whitney.

"We wanted to do everything right," Harriot explains.

On the day of their trip, they geared up and hiked towards Consolation Lake, their first night's camping destination. It was late September, and the weather was cool and dry. Many other hikers were scrambling up the trail that day, and as Harriot and Catherine climbed, they couldn't help noticing the really bad gear some people carried.

"We were shocked by the carelessness and bad planning of the other backpackers," Harriot remembers. "We saw somebody wearing flip flops, someone else with a daypack from Target, and we passed some guys who were trying to summit that day and the only thing they packed was beer. We were thinking, who are these people? This is one of the tallest mountains in the United States. This is a serious hike."

The day grew cooler and Harriot worried about one pair of backpackers in particular. They were a young couple who were "totally inappropriately dressed," she says. The husband had taken off his jacket to give to his cold, crying wife. He was hiking in a white button-down dress shirt that was completely soaked with sweat. His shivering sweetheart wore flimsy canvas sneakers. As the cold weather turned into heavy rain, she pulled out a Mickey Mouse rain poncho. "It looked like something she'd gotten for the flume ride at Disneyland," Harriot says.

The two women forged ahead, arriving at Consolation Lake in the afternoon. Not too long after they set up camp, they saw the poorly prepared couple struggling up the trail and offered to let them camp nearby. "Basically, we wanted to try to convince them to head back down the mountain and not go any farther up," Harriot says.

The couple gratefully accepted Harriot's invitation and began setting up their tent, which they had never done before. They flailed around as they pounded in stakes. They pulled out their sleeping bags, which were flannel bags that weighed a dozen pounds each, and set up a heavy two-burner Coleman stove. When the wife crept to the lake to get water for cooking, Harriot asked her, "Do you have a water filter?" She responded with, "What's that?"

Harriot was dumbfounded. "The whole thing was just a comedy," she says. Harriot filtered water for the couple, helped the husband set up their camp, and gave them some of her extra rain gear. Then she and Catherine retired to their camp to enjoy the evening, relax, and make supper.

They pulled out their brand new, top-of-the-line, ultralight Firefly backpacking stove, set it up under the tent vestibule to protect it from the rain, and hit the igniter. With the first spark, the stove exploded into fire. Fuel spilled everywhere, and their tent nearly went up in flames. In a panic, the women threw sand over the stove. The fuel hose had leaked, causing the fire.

"As we looked at the melted puddle that used to be a fuel hose and the stove which was now useless, we realized that when we got ready for our trip, we didn't check the stove. We thought we were so prepared and perfect, but now we were looking at uncooked top ramen as the highlight of our meal," she says. But then she remembered her camping neighbors. She swallowed her pride and asked the couple for help. "They had a stove. Granted, it was a 500-pound stove, but it was a working stove." The women cooked a hot meal, ate dinner, and went to sleep.

The next morning, Harriot and Catherine rose early, broke down camp, left their neighbors behind, and continued hiking to the top of Mt. Whitney. That day, the weather turned sour. At the summit, it was a whiteout blizzard. They had to stop and wait for the storm to pass, and even though they had acclimated to the elevation, they still felt sick from the altitude. On the way back to the trailhead, the rain was torrential. "We ended up using every piece of gear we brought with us to stay dry," Harriot recalls.

"We were humbled by the whole trip. This was a great reminder to never think you know everything just because you've done it before," she says. "Be humbled by the fact that humans don't naturally do well in the wilderness. You can be as smug as you want, but unless you check and re-check your gear, you shouldn't go anywhere."

5
Water and Food

Satisfying Thirst

You've probably heard that your body is made mostly of water. Men's bodies, in fact, are about 60 percent water and women's bodies are about 55 percent. Even a light exercise session can deplete that percentage, so we need to consume a certain amount of water every day to function at our best. The exact amount is a huge subject of debate because it varies by age, gender, physical activity, and environment.

Here's the standard recommendation (even though it's more of a fuzzy guideline than an evidence-proven rule): an adult male needs about three liters of water per day, and an adult female needs about 2.2 liters per day under normal conditions—i.e., in moderate weather conditions and when we are NOT exercising.

For those who aren't metric-literate, one liter equals roughly thirty-four ounces, meaning one liter equals a little more than four eight-ounce glasses of water. That's how people came up with the notion of drinking a minimum of eight glasses of water per day (and that's under non-exercise conditions).

Exercise intensity and high temperatures increase your daily water needs exponentially.

Many of us don't drink nearly that much, and yet we still thrive. Why? Much of our water requirement is obtained from food, up to 25 percent. Food takes a big bite out of the 2.2- to three-liter water requirement.

Still, most of us go through life with a mild case of dehydration. Our bodies are accustomed to this sorry state of affairs, but that doesn't mean we're performing at our peak levels. Drinking more water means having a better chance at peak performance.

Water serves a number of essential functions in the human body, and some of these functions are particularly essential to our ability to perform physical exercise, that is, to hike. Water regulates our internal body temperature through sweating and respiration. It assists in flushing waste through urination. It acts as a shock absorber for the brain and spinal cord. It lubricates joints. It metabolizes and transports the carbohydrates and proteins that our bodies need for fuel.

So if water is so darn great, why doesn't everyone drink more? When you're hiking, sometimes the problem is simple forgetfulness. It's easy to get distracted by the scenery and the fun of being outdoors, and then forget to drink until you're long past thirsty.

There's a two-pronged solution to that problem: First, hydrate BEFORE you start hiking. The standard advice is to start drinking about two hours before you exercise. As you put on your hiking shoes and socks, drink water. As you drive to the trailhead, drink water. Ann Marie is famous among her hiking friends for downing a big bottle of water, plus a bottle of her homemade kombucha, plus maybe a triple-shot nonfat latte, all while she drives to the trailhead. She's also famous for having to pee the second she gets out of the car. But she isn't dehydrated.

Then there's Part Two of the hydration solution, and that's to continually sip fluids as you exercise (rather than gulping down an entire bottle when you finally stop for a trail break). It's easy enough to accomplish this on a day-hike: drink the contents of two standard-size, one-liter water bottles (like the Nalgene or REI brands of wide-mouth bottles that many hikers carry), and you'll take in about seventy fluid ounces. If you do this, and you've already sucked up a bunch of water before your day-hike and gulped down more when you're done, you're going to feel great. On a backpack trip, you should try to drink that same quantity every day, or even more. The good news is that you'll probably have "wet" meals at breakfast and dinner, which will help you to hydrate. It might be oatmeal cooked in water for breakfast, or soup or stew cooked in water at dinner. You'll get a good amount of water from your camp-cooked meals if you're cooking with water.

The problem with water is that it's heavy. One liter of water equals about 2.2 pounds of weight. Carry two liters and you're looking at 4.4 pounds. Carry three liters and you're looking at almost seven pounds. Day-hikers may be willing to put up with that kind of weight, but backpackers moan and wail and wring their hands at the thought of hefting seven additional pounds. With that kind of extra weight, why not carry your espresso maker, too?

Instead of loading yourself up like a pack mule, plan your trip around water sources, and carry a purification device so you can get clean, safe water wherever you go. More on that in the upcoming section, "Making Natural Water Safe to Drink."

How Much Is Too Much?

All this talk about drinking water begs the question: is it possible to drink too much? The answer is yes, but this happens only very rarely. The opposite of dehydration is hyponatremia. With this condition, sodium levels in the blood become so diluted by too much water that cellular function is impaired. You may have heard media reports about a few triathletes and ultra-long-distance runners lapsing into comas or even dying from hyponatremia. Could it happen to you? It's pretty unlikely unless you're subsisting on an almost all-water diet. In places like the Grand Canyon or Death Valley, where every trail sign you see and every ranger you meet reminds you to drink water, you'll also learn this caveat to the water rule: keep your sodium levels balanced by eating a salty snack when you stop for a water break. Another way to balance your sodium levels is to drink a sports drink that contains electrolytes, but we prefer plain old water and a couple of pretzels.

Hydration Packs

One of the easiest ways to stay hydrated is to use a backpack-style hydration system, the kind with a hose straw that allows you to easily access your water, even while hiking. With a hydration pack, you don't have to stop hiking to pull out your water bottle. Water is always in reach of your lips. You can sip as you saunter, run, meander, or trudge. Just make sure you're carrying at least seventy fluid ounces or two liters for a short day hike, and even more if you're going to be out all day, or if the weather is especially hot or dry.

CamelBak is probably the most famous of the hydration pack manufacturers, but Osprey, MSR, and many other companies make excellent hydration packs as well. You can buy a reservoir only (also called a bladder, and they come in one-, two-, or three-liter sizes) that fits into the back "sleeve" of your existing backpack or day-pack. This works just fine as long as your pack is fairly new—and by new we mean that you bought it in the last decade, when pack companies starting making packs with reservoir sleeves. Just make sure the reservoir you buy fits with your particular pack—they aren't "one-size-fits-all."

Or if you're shopping for a new pack anyway, you can buy a hiker-specific hydration pack, with a reservoir that is custom-built inside the pack.

If you already own and use a hydration pack, you must give it some maintenance now and then. Ditto for any water bottle that you carry. Most people can remember to clean their water bottles (or at least toss them in the dishwasher occasionally), but somehow forget to clean their hydration packs. Leaving liquid, even if it is plain water, in your hydration pack reservoir is a recipe for cultivating an interstellar galaxy of bacteria and mold.

In a perfect world, you would drain, rinse, and air-dry your hydration bladder after every use. In the world that Ann Marie lives in, she finishes a hike and tosses her pack in the backseat of her Subaru. It's unpleasant to imagine what occurs inside that reservoir while it sits in her sunbaked car for a few days.

The key to keeping your reservoir from growing funky stuff inside is to wash it fairly often, and even more important, dry it thoroughly. To wash your reservoir, fill it with hot water and two tablespoons of baking soda. If you're a clean freak, you can use bleach or isopropyl alcohol instead, or borrow some of Grandma's denture-cleaning tablets. Polident works great, but don't forget to replace Grandma's stash.

With the cleaning solution inside, shake your bladder a bunch of times, let it sit for a half-hour, then shake some more. Hang it up on a clothes hanger or a shower curtain rod (or a tree branch, or whatever) and squeeze the bite valve so the baking soda/bleach/Polident water runs out. Make sure you rinse the bladder and flush the hose several times with fresh water so you don't taste your cleaning solution next time you use it. (If you aren't a do-it-yourselfer, CamelBak sells a cleaning kit for $20, which has some brushes, a hanger, and cleaning tablets.)

The drying process is the most important part. You don't want any moisture trapped inside because moisture is a mold incubator. Hanging your reservoir is the best way to air-dry it. Terra puts a ruler or a stick inside hers to force open its collapsible sides while it dries.

If you aren't going to use your reservoir for a while, store it in the freezer. Even if there's a little bit of moisture left in it, mold can't grow in freezer temperatures.

Making Natural Water Safe to Drink

If you're heading out for an all-day hike, two liters may not be nearly enough water, especially in hot weather or at high elevation. If you're backpacking, there's no question about it—you're going to need to find a way to refill those bottles, unless you think carrying ten gallons of water on your back is a good idea.

Always carry a water filtering device so you can refill your water bottle at streams, rivers, or lakes—or even putrid-smelling mud puddles if the need arises (and if you hike enough miles in your lifetime, the need will probably arise).

No matter how clear and fresh natural water may look, don't drink water from a natural source without purifying it. Gulping fresh water from a crystalline mountain stream sounds delightful on a hot day, but it's less delightful when you end up running for the bushes every ten minutes for the next two weeks. The microscopic organisms *giardia lamblia* and *cryptosporidium* are found in natural water sources and can cause a litany of nasty gastrointestinal problems. Nasty as in diarrhea. Nasty as in you may fart for months.

How do these illness-causing bugs get into streams and lakes in beautiful backcountry areas? Here's a clue: Canadians call giardiasis, the illness caused by *giardia,* "beaver fever." Water sources become contaminated when feces containing the *giardia* or *cryptosporidium* organisms are deposited into the water. So, whether it's a beaver, or a dog, or a human, or a cow, if anything or anyone has pooped in or near a natural water source, the water may be contaminated. They don't have to poop directly into your lake or stream, either. They may have pooped somewhere upstream from where you are scooping water, and the contaminants have floated downstream to your water bottle.

Only purifying or boiling water from natural sources will eliminate *giardiasis* and *cryptosporidiosis.* Fortunately, there are lots of ways to make water from natural sources safe to drink, starting with the most low-tech solution: fire. If you have a backcountry stove or a campfire, you can boil backcountry water. After one full minute at a rapid boil—or three minutes if you're above 6,000 feet—your water will be safe from *giardia* and *cryptosporidium,* plus any other disease-causing microorganisms that might be present. Your water will be safe, but it's also hot as hell, so boiling is a good solution only if you are making tea, coffee, or soup. If you want to drink cold water

Boiling water is one way to eliminate giardiasis and cryptosporidiosis, but it's not the most efficient way.

because you are thirsty right now, well, plan on a long wait for that boiled water to cool.

Water Bottle–Style Purifiers

Or try a slighter higher-tech solution. Water bottle–style purifiers, such as those made by Sawyer, Katadyn, GRAYL, or CamelBak, are as light as an empty plastic bottle and eliminate the need to carry both a filter and a bottle. You simply dip the bottle in the stream, screw on the top (which has a filter inside it), and squeeze the bottle to drink. The water is filtered on its way out of the squeeze top and into your mouth.

Sawyer makes two models, the Squeeze and the Mini, which are particularly clever. They come with three collapsible bag-like bottles of different sizes, so you save on the bulk of carrying a Nalgene or other water bottle. The Sawyer Squeeze and the Mini are simple to use, long lasting, small, lightweight, and affordable at $25 to $50. The Mini weighs only 1.8 ounces for the filter and a collapsible bag bottle, and so has become a favorite of ultralight backpackers.

The upsides to these water bottle–style purifiers are easy to see. There are a couple of downsides, though. If you don't screw the top on properly, or if unfiltered lake or stream water drips down the sides of the bottle and into your mouth, you could still get sick. Also, you're only filtering one bottle at a time, which may be fine for day-hiking when you need a quick drink, but it's nowhere near enough water for backpacking when you need a lot of water to cook dinner for a group.

Ultraviolet Light Filters: the SteriPEN

So consider the next step up in the high-tech world of water safety. It will cost you about $100, but many hikers, including us, swear by a contraption called SteriPEN, which uses ultraviolet light rays instead of chemicals to purify water. It's small, light, runs on batteries, and purifies thirty-two ounces of water in about ninety seconds. You hold the handle, press the "on" button, insert the lightbulb in the neck of your water bottle, swirl it around, and voilá—you have water that's safe to drink.

A few important considerations with the SteriPEN: you need to make sure you carry a wide-mouth water bottle so the lightbulb will fit inside the neck. Most hikers use these anyway, so that's probably not a big deal. But what could be a very big deal is that the SteriPEN runs on batteries, and as we all know, batteries seem to die when we need them most. So always carry spare batteries for your SteriPEN. And yes, batteries are heavy, so figure on a few ounces of total extra weight with the SteriPEN and an extra set of batteries. Is it worth it for easy access to clean water? We think so.

The only other part that may go kaput on the SteriPEN is the bulb or lamp, which is intended to last for 10,000 uses. Ann Marie's died one day when she was on a simple day-hike, but fortunately she was hiking with someone else who also had a StreriPEN. The lesson:

The SteriPEN uses ultraviolet light to make water safe to drink.

Carry more than one SteriPEN per group, or carry one SteriPEN and one other kind of water purifier. When Ann Marie goes on long solo hikes, she carries a SteriPEN and a LifeStraw (see page 131). So far she's never had to use the LifeStraw, but she likes knowing she has built-in redundancy.

Traditional hikers insist on tried-and-true hand-pump filters, like those made by Katadyn or MSR. Ann Marie used these for ages before she got her first SteriPEN, but that purchase was a game-changer. Granted, it can be pleasantly zen-like to sit along-side an alpine lake pumping water through a filter, but it can also be boring. The more people you're making coffee for, the greater the boredom.

John Kleinfelter is a wilderness guide. When he takes families or groups out on backpack trips, he always carries a SteriPEN for purifying water on the trail and a Katadyn pump filter for purifying water in camp. He also carries a collapsible bucket, so he can scoop up a couple of gallons of lake or stream water and carry it back to camp for pumping. Just recently he graduated from the hand-style pump to the Katadyn Gravity filter, which hangs from a tree branch and doesn't require pumping. Good-bye, carpal tunnel syndrome; gravity does all the work. The Gravity weighs in at twelve ounces, and Katadyn's regular hand-pump filters, the Hiker or Hiker Pro, weigh eleven ounces, so there's not a lot of difference. The Gravity is an effortless way to always have enough water for a big group.

Pumping water through a ceramic filter is the dependable "old school" method to filter water for drinking.

A collapsible bucket makes it easy to carry a lot of water to camp and then filter it as you need it.

LifeStraw

For solo hikers or couples who want to go ultralight, there's a plastic "straw" that purifies water so you can drink right out of creeks and lakes. The LifeStraw Personal Water Filter could be a lifesaver in a survival situation, and it's become a favorite purification device for many minimalist backpackers. It costs about $20, fits in your pocket, and weighs only two ounces. It doesn't need batteries, so it's fairly foolproof. It doesn't use chemicals, so the filtered water always tastes great. To use it, you simply uncap the bottom, place it in a lake or stream, and sip through the top. If you don't feel like lying on the ground right next to the water, you can fill up a water bottle and insert the filter to start sipping.

Some hikers complain that you have to suck pretty hard on the straw to get the flow going. Our hiking friend Joe Stimper, who swears by the LifeStraw, says he gets much better suction when he's sitting and has the straw inserted in a water bottle, rather than lying on the ground drinking out of a lake. He thinks he can generate more suction in the upright position. He also says it helps if he keeps his water bottle mostly full. The emptier it gets, the harder he has to suck, so in between sips, he dips his bottle in the lake to fill it.

There are no moving parts in the LifeStraw, and it requires almost no maintenance. After every use, you should blow out any residual water to prevent clogging and keep the filter clean. It's guaranteed to work for 260 gallons, or about 1,000 liters of water.

Iodine Tablets

If you don't want to deal with the weight, bulk, and cost of a water filter, you could choose iodine tablets as your water purification device. It's an ultralight option, and it's also the traditionalist's choice. You fill a bottle with lake or stream water, drop in an iodine tablet, wait thirty minutes, and drink. It's cheap and weighs next to nothing, but this is our least favorite water-purifying choice. We don't like that iodine tablets are not effective against *cryptosporidium* (but they do eliminate *giardia*). We don't like the thirty-minute wait required before you can drink. But most of all, we don't like that the tablets make sweet mountain water taste like chemicals. Some people add a "taste neutralizer tablet" or crushed vitamin-C pill to bring the taste back to something approximating normal.

Opinions are like belly buttons. Everybody has one. But in order of preference, here are Terra and Ann Marie's top choices for water purification devices:

For one or two hikers: the Steri-PEN and LifeStraw combination. If you're a maverick who is obsessed with saving weight, choose one or the other, not both. If you're a worry-wort like Terra, carry both.

For groups of three or more: Katadyn Gravity filter.

How Much Is Enough?

So how do you know if you're taking in enough water? Obvious signs of dehydration include fatigue, dry mouth, and headache, followed by cramps and nausea. But these symptoms could be signs of other problems, like altitude sickness or heat exhaustion, so they aren't the best test. A sure-fire test for dehydration is simply to pay attention to your urine when you pee. Ideally, you should pee often and heartily when you are hiking. Ever hear of the saying "pee like a racehorse"? That's the hiker's mantra, but if you prefer something more scientific, you can use "copious and clear"; meaning your urine should be light in color and high in volume.

Electrolytes

Some hikers say that no matter how much water they drink, they still end up feeling depleted after a few hours on the trail. They find themselves eating snacks to bolster their energy, but that doesn't seem to work, either. One solution is to pack along not just water but also some type of sports drink or energy drink, one that will help restore carbohydrates and electrolytes. Many of these drinks are now available in powdered form, so backpackers can sip an electrolyte-rich drink even when they are three days from the nearest grocery store.

On longer day-hikes or backpacking trips, Ann Marie tends to get bored with drinking plain old water all the time. She always brings along something to add to her water bottle. Plain water is what she drinks most of the time, but at the end of a long climb, or at dinnertime on a backpacking trip, she often reaches for her "cocktail" mix. It might be dehydrated coconut water or just a simple dried lemonade mix—anything that will provide readily available carbohydrate energy to working muscles and replenish electrolytes.

Companies like Vitalyte, Skratch Labs, and Hammer Nutrition make electrolyte mixes that are scientifically formulated, but we'd rather skip the lab-created drinks and go with plain old coconut water. If you do choose to go with a commercial mix, check the ingredient list to make sure it contains sodium chloride, citrate, bicarbonate, monopotassium phosphate, dipotassium phosphate, or l-lactate—all of these are components of electrolytes. It should also have a high percentage of carbohydrates.

Your Water Plan for Extended Trips

Day-hikers can usually carry enough water for their hikes unless they're hiking in an area where it is extremely hot. But backpackers need a lot more than one day's worth of water, so that requires some planning. Where are the water sources on your planned trail? Is there water close to where you'll be camping? How much water do you need to get from one source to the next?

Hikers sometimes encounter problems when they depend on finding a water source that is shown on the map. What if the environmental conditions have changed since the map was drawn? Desert springs can dry up, and even high-mountain springs can disappear. What if the map is wrong, or worse yet, what if you read the map incorrectly? Sometimes when you think you have a good plan for finding water, things can go wrong. Poor decision-making can leave you thirsty—and thirst can lead to a risky situation.

Kip Myers found that out the hard way on an extended backpacking trip in the Sierra. He and his friends were on the third day of their trip and faced a demanding climb to 12,000-foot Shepherd Pass, where they would enter Sequoia National Park and then climb Mount Tyndall and Mount Russell. The trail is notoriously difficult, with steep grades and lots of loose talus.

"Shepherd Pass goes from down low to way up high. You start in the desert sagebrush at about 6,000 feet, and you climb up to Shepherd Pass at 12,000 feet," Kip says.

The group's plan was to get to Shepherd Pass in one hard day, covering about twelve miles. Their packs were heavy and they knew what they were in for.

"We started early, probably 6 a.m., because we knew it was going to be hot. We didn't want to carry a lot of water because we had a lot of hard climbing to do. We had looked at the map, and we saw that Shepherd Creek followed the trail almost all the way, so we figured we'd just stop and get water any time we wanted it," he recalls.

"We started climbing up, and it got hotter and hotter. There was no shade at all, and we couldn't get out of the sun. Our packs felt really heavy. We each had a bottle of water, but we drank that really quickly. We figured, no problem, we'll be at the creek soon and we can refill our bottles," Kip says.

"What we didn't pay attention to when we read the map was that there were a whole bunch of contour lines between our trail and the creek. The trail goes along the cliff's edge, and the creek is at the bottom of the cliff. In between was a scree slope with lots of loose rock. We could have gotten down to the water, but then we would have had to climb back up to the trail."

The friends kept debating whether they should descend the difficult scree slope to get water, then come back to the trail, or just keep walking until they reached a spot where the water was easier to reach.

"We were so hot that nobody could bear the thought of adding on that extra trip. We just wanted to get up higher as soon as possible, where we knew it would be cooler. We all were getting really dehydrated. It was torture because we could see the water the whole time, and every five minutes one of us would say, 'We gotta go get that water,' but we couldn't bear the thought of doing it."

The men started to have trouble reasoning. "We were totally focused on getting to the top of Shepherd Pass as soon as possible," Kip says, "even though now it makes no sense. We were stumbling along, and my brother twisted his ankle, but we kept slogging. We were even talking about throwing food out of our packs to make them lighter, but then somebody said, 'Yeah, but if we do that, what are we going to eat?' Our brains were barely functioning. We were not thinking clearly at all.

"Finally we made it to Anvil Camp, about ten miles up the trail, where the creek and the trail finally met up. We were all pretty screwed up by the time we made it. We laid our packs down and just about passed out by the creek. We just lay there and drank and drank and drank. Of course we never made it to Shepherd Pass that day anyway," he says.

Kip says it's easy to sum up that day's big lesson: "I never go anywhere without carrying a ton of water. I never assume I'll be able to find it."

Finding Water in the Desert

Finding water in the mountains or in coastal areas isn't usually too difficult, but what if Murphy's Law comes into play when you're hiking in the desert? What if you knock over all your water bottles, or you get lost in a canyon in triple-digit heat? The good news is that even a person who runs out of water in extreme heat conditions can survive for up to forty-eight hours by managing his or her own body temperature and sweat. Finding shade is the key priority. Don't try to wander around between 10 a.m. and 4 p.m. and find a way out of the mess you're in. Hole up and wait for help. Keep your skin covered from the sun, and stay out of the wind if possible.

Barrel cactus are a classic icon of the desert, but don't try to obtain drinking water from them; their liquid is poisonous.

It's possible to find water in many areas of the desert, but don't try the classic Western cartoon maneuver—lopping the top off a barrel cactus. The water inside most cacti is filled with alkalis that will make you much sicker than not having water at all. However, almost all types of cactus have edible fruit. The well-known prickly pear cactus bears thumb-sized fruits that contain about 85 percent water, so that's a step in the right direction. But you'd have to eat hundreds of these fruits to make a dent in your hydration needs, and many types of prickly pear fruits need to be de-spined before they can be eaten. Cholla flowers are also edible, but getting to the flowers without getting poked is a formidable task. So forget about cactus.

Instead, look for bright green, broad-leafed trees like cottonwoods and willows, or in the few American deserts where palm trees grow—Anza-Borrego, Joshua Tree, Mojave, and near Palm Springs—look for native palm oases. The only palm native to North America, the

Palm trees are often fed by underground springs, so you can usually find water in the ground somewhere near their trunks.

California fan palm (*Washingtonia filifera*) provides life-giving shade and is a key indicator that water is nearby. Cottonwoods, willows, and palms are usually fed by underground springs, so there's often water on the surface somewhere near their trunks. It will probably be nasty, murky, stagnant water, but that's what water filters are made for. If you can't find a water hole near a cottonwood or willow or palm, start digging down toward its roots. The hole you've dug will soon fill up with water.

Just ask Rosie Hackett, who worked as an outdoor educator with Colorado Outward Bound. When she was twenty-four years old, Rosie and another instructor led a group of ten teenagers on a ten-day excursion into the sculpted, red rock canyons of southwest Utah's vast desert. Rosie's job was to teach rock climbing and back-packing skills to the amateur hikers.

"We decided to go on a new route through Bodie Canyon," Rosie remembers. She had never ventured into Bodie Canyon before, but she had heard that the terrain was technical and difficult. She planned the route, and with the help of her course directors, marked on the map all the designated water sources.

"Water is always an issue at that time of year. However, we did some reconnaissance missions earlier in the summer and saw where the water was in the area."

The group began their trek in Bodie Canyon, heading deep into the desert. With only sandstone walls and boulders lining the canyon, there was little shade. The intense sun baked them as they hiked. "We were getting acclimatized to the heat," Rosie says, "as we were moving several miles through the canyon every day."

Each person toted a heavy backpack loaded with three quart-sized water-bottles and one six-quart dromedary bag, which they refilled every time they discovered water.

"Whenever we found a water hole, it was amazing. We would immediately jump in it," Rosie says.

Rosie and her gaggle of teenagers spent their mornings hiking through the canyon while the air was cool. Around noon, when the sun reached its peak and the heat became unbearable, they would rest in the shade. "We'd try to find a watering hole where we would chug tons of water before moving on," Rosie says.

On the fifth day, the group hiked all morning and into the afternoon, pushing through the sweltering midday heat in search of a water source. They had dry-camped for the previous two nights and were running dangerously low on water. "We each had less than one quart of water left and nothing in our dromedaries. It was scary," Rosie says.

Following her map of Bodie Canyon, Rosie urged her students to hike onward towards a water source that was shown on the map. When they arrived, they found a dry, cracked mud flat.

"On my map, this was shown to be a big watering hole," Rosie explains. "But when we finally got there, nowhere in the vicinity was there any water."

With deflated spirits, the group crumpled on the ground, not knowing what to do next. "I looked at my students and co-instructor, and they looked completely hot and exhausted," Rosie remembers. "Everyone was saying, 'We can't go any farther. We're going to die.'"

Although Rosie was carrying a satellite phone, there was no way to call for help. For the phone to get even a faint signal, the group needed to climb out of the canyon. To do so would require an immense amount of physical exertion, and they simply didn't have enough water for the task.

Rosie's co-instructor was suffering from heat exhaustion, so Rosie knew she had to act. She realized it was her responsibility to get those kids out of the desert alive. "I was feeling like I needed to rise up to the occasion and find water in that canyon," Rosie says. "If I didn't, I could kill twelve people, including myself."

Turning to her scared students, she said, "I need someone to come with me." No one volunteered. Then, a thin, freckled arm popped up and a small voice chirped, "I'll go with you, Rosie." It was Timmy, the weakest link in the group chain.

"He was the smallest, skinniest, most insecure kid," Rosie recalls. "He'd had trouble adapting the whole time and was a mess, always losing stuff and messing up on things. But I looked at him and said, 'Great, you're coming!'"

To prepare for their mission, Rosie and Timmy collected all the water bottles and combined what was left of the precious liquid—only five quarts for the whole group. Each took two quarts, left the rest for the others, and loaded their backpacks with empty dromedary bags. Then, with Rosie leading the way, the duo headed out, intent on locating a water source.

The twisting canyon was exposed to the sun and strewn with huge boulders. "We hiked for about two miles, which probably took us four hours. It was slow, technical hiking, or as I call it 'four-wheel-driving' because you are using all four limbs," Rosie explains.

Rosie became more and more fatigued. Timmy, on the other hand, trotted behind her, chattering incessantly and in seemingly good shape. "Rosie! Rosie! Are we going to find water? Are we going to die? Are we going to kill everybody?"

Rosie couldn't reply. She was suffering from dehydration and heat exhaustion, and each step forward took momentous effort. "We had already drank both quarts of water," Rosie recalls. "Timmy was a teenager and didn't need much water, so he was doing fine. But he was starting to get nervous because I wasn't communicating with him."

Rosie grew even weaker and was barely plodding forward when they rounded a bend in the canyon. She looked up, squinting in the harsh light. What she saw made her nearly weep with relief. "I saw this amazing cottonwood, this massive tree with green foliage and tons of shade, which in the desert is the most beautiful thing," Rosie says. "I was thinking, there's water, I know there's water right there. Nothing can grow like that in the desert unless there's a water source."

Scrambling over boulders, they rushed towards the tree, which shimmered in the sunlight. At its base lay a small pool of water, about twelve feet across and three feet deep, surrounded by thick reeds. Globs of brown algae and wiggling tadpoles drifted across its stagnant, muddy surface. The hikers threw off their backpacks and collapsed on the ground in relief.

"We got down on our hands and knees. I felt so happy,'" Rosie remembers.

They strained the thick, murky water through a filter into their water bottles, then they dropped purification tablets into them. The iodine tablets took twenty minutes to purify the liquid. "We waited, and then he and I just started chugging. We chugged three or four bottles of water before we did anything," Rosie says.

After hydrating, they filled the empty dromedary bags, and with loaded packs and high spirits, hiked back to the group. When they reached the others, it was late afternoon and the students were lying on the ground, wilted. They had no more water left. Rosie's co-instructor was very sick.

"They did not look good," Rosie recalls. "They were all still lying down, but when they saw us, they got up."

Rosie pulled out the bursting dromedary bags, and with a flourish, filled everyone's water bottles. Clinking their bottles together in a salute, the students gulped the life-saving liquid. "It was like a party. We hung out and hydrated, then moved our camp to the cottonwood tree."

The remaining days of the canyon trek went smoothly. Rosie led the group through Bodie Canyon, finding a new water source each day, and her bumbling student Timmy was no longer the weakest link. "He had been the one who struggled and never could do anything right," Rosie says. "For the rest of the course, everyone saw him in a different light. Timmy became the hero."

And ever since that trip there's a special place in Rosie's heart for the bright leafy green of a cottonwood tree.

Food for Hiking and Backpacking

Every time you see a movie about someone who gets lost in the wilderness, the first thing the lost hero or heroine does is make a trap for catching a rabbit or a squirrel, or catch fish with his or her bare hands, or do some similar Hollywood nonsense.

Movies are fun to watch, but they're fictitious. If you're lost in the wilderness, you have a lot bigger priorities than what's for dinner. First and foremost, you need shelter and water. Food? Well, it would be really nice if you happened to have a Costco-sized box of protein bars in your pack, but if you don't, you'll be able to live for two to three weeks off the fat stores in your body. Even if you're already pretty skinny.

On the other hand, if you run out of water, you'll probably die in three to five days.

Food is important. Food makes your body work better. Food plus water translates into energy. Food may help you to make better decisions. Food helps your mood and your attitude. But if you have to, you can live for a long time without it.

Still, like most hikers, we love to eat. If you looked in our packs before a day-hike, you'd be astounded at the array of food. If you looked in our packs before a backpacking trip, you'd think we were feeding a fraternity of linebackers and their pet wolves, not two medium-sized women.

Ann Marie has always remembered the sad misfortune of the backpacking trip she took at age nineteen, when she and her equally

Food plus water translates into energy.

inexperienced college friends ran out of food on the third day of a planned four-day trip. Everybody felt crabby. There was a lot of blaming and finger-pointing. The group hiked out a day early, gorged on hamburgers in the nearest town, and salvaged their friendship. Now you'll never find Ann Marie without snacks—in her car, in her backpack, in her pockets, sometimes even stuffed into her extra pair of socks.

But to illustrate how well the body can function without food, meet Brian Gass. First, some background: Brian is a bad-ass hiker. He doesn't hike the way most of us do. In his world, a leisurely day-hike is twenty-five miles long with 5,000 feet of elevation gain.

In the summer of 2014, twenty-one-year-old Gass conquered the Pacific Crest Trail (PCT), a 2,659-mile trail that traverses through three states, twenty-five national forests, and seven national parks. Essentially, he walked from Mexico to Canada. He started at the California/Mexico border and trekked north through the desert, covering significant ground every day.

"The desert is the hardest section of the PCT because you're getting into hiking and your body is getting used to the struggle. You get physically and mentally toughened," Brian says.

In June, Brian reached the foothills of the Sierra Nevada Mountains. By that time, he was already 1,000 miles deep on the PCT and accustomed to long trail days. But conditions were different in the Sierra. Snow fields still covered the passes and the meadows were soggy with spring snowmelt.

Brian stopped in Kennedy Meadows, California, to bolster his food supply before ascending to higher elevations. The pack station and cabin resort at Kennedy Meadows is a one-stop shop for hikers on the PCT, where they can mail packages, pick up provisions, and relax before rejoining the trail.

"I got tons of food and was excited to just hang out, rest up, and get ready to go into the Sierra," Brian recalls. After a couple days, he returned to the PCT with a loaded backpack. His food canister was stuffed with peanut butter, tuna, tortillas, cheese, and nuts. "It was all really high-calorie food," he says. "I remember leaving Kennedy

Meadows and thinking my backpack was really heavy. I was ready for anything."

He decided that instead of stopping at the next re-supply station, he would hike through to Vermillion Valley Resort, which was 176 miles away. Most hikers break up this section of the PCT with a pit stop in Bishop, California. But not Brian. He figured he could cover those 176 miles in under a week.

"I am notorious for biting off more than I can chew," he says. "I decided to do a larger section of the trail. I thought I had enough food and wanted to take on the challenge."

Brian trekked onward through the Sierra. In the distance, he could see Mount Whitney's snowy summit jutting through the clouds. At 14,505 feet, Whitney is the highest peak in the lower forty-eight states, and most who trek to its summit spend months preparing to climb its precipitous trail. But again, not Brian. Even though Mount Whitney is several miles off the PCT, he decided to summit the mountain for fun. "I saw it and thought, *I have to do this*. So I went up Mount Whitney," he says.

Climbing Whitney added an extra day to his itinerary and depleted a lot more of his food than he had anticipated. But Brian forged ahead on the PCT, traversing the numerous mountain passes that separated him from Vermillion Valley Resort. But he wasn't making good time. The California sunshine was warming the Sierra Nevada, and at high elevations, the trail was covered in mushy snow. "I'd punch deeper and deeper until the snow was up to my thighs. If I was wearing shorts, it would cut my legs," Brian says. "Because I was post-holing in the snow, I over-estimated my mileage."

On his fifth day out of Kennedy Meadows, Brian realized he was going to run out of provisions before he reached his next resupply station. He began to ration his food.

"When I'm hiking, I try to eat between 3,000 and 5,000 calories a day. I had to ration that down to 1,000 calories a day," he says. "And at that point my body was so efficient at burning calories that I went into starvation mode."

Even though Brian had incredible physical endurance, it was challenging to hike on an empty stomach. He stopped enjoying the scenery and began dreaming of food. "I was in the most beautiful place on earth and all I could think about was a cheeseburger," he says.

After four days of eating not nearly enough calories, Brian finally reached the trail leading to Vermillion Valley Resort. It was only eight more miles to the store. His cell phone, which hadn't had a signal for weeks, suddenly had service. He called the resort to see how late it would be open.

"They told me they closed in thirty minutes," Brian says. "I asked them to wait for me, and I sprinted, running full-speed for eight miles."

The restaurant stayed open, and Brian collapsed at a table as a waitress approached. "She told me I was skinny and needed to eat. I have always been a big guy, and nobody's ever told me that. But I probably lost fifteen pounds in those nine days."

He ordered a bacon double-cheeseburger and a milkshake. "It was the best food in the world," Brian says.

Brian admits that he probably should have gotten off the trail earlier to resupply, but because everything turned out okay for him, he doesn't have any regrets. "It was hard going without food, but I was fine. I think if you don't push yourself to the limits, you're missing out on seeing what you're capable of."

Brian is an uber-athlete, so he shrugs off his going-hungry experience as just another day on the trail. Most of us aren't nearly as badass as Brian, but we do have a similar capacity to function with very little food. Even people who aren't overweight carry enough body fat to subsist for two to three weeks without any food at all.

Run out of water and you'll probably die in three to five days. But run out of food and you'll feel cranky and dream of cheeseburgers. You may think you're losing your mind, but you'll stay alive.

What Food to Bring

If you're day-hiking, you can bring darn near anything you want to eat, as long as it won't spoil in the day's heat. Sometimes Terra will even bring food that must stay cold—like a sandwich with lots of mayonnaise. She'll just pack it in her day-pack with a couple of freezer packs.

Day-hikers can afford food luxuries since they only need to carry enough for one day. Hiker John Gateman once carried a full sixteen-ounce jar of peanut butter, a glass jar of strawberry jam, and an entire loaf of bread to the top of Half Dome in Yosemite National Park. He didn't have time to make a PB&J sandwich before he left home, so he just brought everything with him and handed out sandwiches to strangers. Another trekker, Mason Brutschy, always carries a can or two of sardines. On day hikes, take whatever floats your boat.

Ideally for both day-hiking and backpacking, you want high calorie and/or high fat foods. When you're exercising for long hours, you can wind up with strong cravings. Ann Marie never knows exactly what she's going to want to eat, so she carries a wide range of sweet and salty foods. Even on day hikes, she usually has one sweet item (like an orange or a package of M&Ms) as well as one salty item (crackers or chips or salted nuts) in addition to more nutritious food, like a turkey sandwich. If she's carrying food for two, she'll bring a bag of pita pocket bread (it doesn't go stale quickly) and a small plastic jar of peanut butter or almond butter. In the bottom of her pack, she always has some nuts and dried fruit—the quintessential hiking foods because they provide energy and fill you up. Commercial "trail mixes"—a yummy mix of nuts and dried fruits and sometimes chocolate—tend to be heavy on the sugar, so she prefers to mix her own.

For backpacking, your food choices should be lightweight, or reasonably so. In addition to all the snack-type foods that you'd carry for day-hiking (nuts, dried fruit, trail mix, etc.), you also need to carry more substantial foods to make meals.

We asked our adventurer friend John Platt to weigh in on his favorite foods for backpacking, and he came up with a three-part answer. Sometimes he goes gourmet and makes elaborate backcountry meals, sometimes he goes minimalist and brings freeze-dried food, and sometimes he does the "total dirt-bag thing," which he describes as "no stove, just granola bars and peanut butter on a spoon."

You won't need any instructions on how to do the "dirt-bag thing," but John was kind enough to share a few of his fancier camp recipes with us.

For dinners, John walks around his local grocery store and pulls out items that are easy to cook in boiling water. His tomato tortellini recipe requires three simple ingredients: one package of dried tortellini, one-half cup of sun-dried tomatoes, and one package of McCormick Italian-style spaghetti sauce mix (a dry mix that comes in an envelope). He brings his water to a boil, adds the tortellini, and boils it for one minute. When the tortellini is about half done, he adds the sauce mix and sun-dried tomatoes, then seasons each serving with garlic salt. You could also use dried basil or rosemary.

John also makes Asian noodles with clams, a dish that he calls "slightly exotic." He packs in a box of rice noodles, two foil packs of clams (find them in your grocery store near the tuna fish), and one package of Sunbird Pad Thai dry sauce mix. He boils the noodles, then adds the clams and sauce mix near the end.

John notes that foil packs of clams and salmon can be a great way to include meat in a backcountry dinner. "They're lighter than a can, and it's easier to pack out the waste," he says. He makes a similar dish with a foil pack of salmon, a package of Knorr pesto sauce, and noodles. He likes rice noodles because they cook quickly. The thicker the noodle, the longer it takes to cook, so leave the rigatoni at home.

John is quick to emphasize what all good backcountry cooks know: spices matter. And these ingredients weigh almost nothing. He always brings some garlic salt, Tabasco, tamari, Spike, and other spices to season individual servings.

John also extols the virtues of the bagel for making pack-sturdy sandwiches. "For a complete meal-in-a-baggie, the bagel sandwich excels," he says. "Unlike wimpy bread, bagels can stand up to the contents inside a backpack and still be recognizable as food."

John is also a fan of the backcountry cookbook *In the Wild Chef* (2015) by Steve Weston, which shows how to make "real food" in the backcountry. Another great cookbook resource is *Lip-Smackin' Backpackin'* (2000) by Tim and Christine Conners.

A backpacking kitchen can be as simple as a slab of granite and your stove and cooking gear.

How Much Food?

Most backpackers need to carry 1.5 to two pounds of food for each day they're hiking. Terra and Ann Marie each do fine with 1.5 pounds per person per day; a larger-size man or a growing teenager would probably need two pounds. Everybody's different in terms of caloric needs; if you don't know how much food you need, go out on a short trip (two or three nights) and try taking two pounds of food per person per day. If you come home with tons of leftover food, reduce that amount in the future.

Of course, the nutrient density of your 1.5 pounds of food makes a big difference. If you take Cheetos, they don't weigh much, but they won't give you much bang for your buck. You also need to consider the unique demands of each trip that you take: if you're planning on multiple long-mileage days, you'll need more food than if you're just sitting around in camp for two days out of four.

Take whatever you want to eat, but to reduce pack weight, choose foods that don't contain water. Many backpackers choose to eat almost nothing but freeze-dried dinners. They weigh almost nothing because all the water has been sucked out during the drying process. You simply add water that you've boiled on your camp stove while you watch the sun go down over Blue Paradise Lake.

We have eaten our fair share of freeze-dried backpacking food, and some of it's pretty good. But some of it's pretty bad. On a longer trip, Ann Marie will carry a few packets of freeze-dried dinners for the nights when she is too tired to do anything but boil water. The only brands she really likes are AlpineAire and Good To-Go, but these are both much more expensive than the standards that have been around for ages, like Mountain House and Backpacker's Pantry. For her, the extra expense is worth it—that higher price tag means less weird chemicals in her dinner.

Always read freeze-dried food labels carefully. Many are low on nutrition but ultra-high on sodium. They're often not high-calorie, either, and when you're hiking, you need calories.

She'll also take her own "soup mixes," which include freeze-dried veggies like sun-dried tomatoes or dried peas and corn (sold in major grocery stores under the trade name Just Veggies), pasta or rice, dried meats or jerky, and most important of all—a pinch of some spice or herb so dinner doesn't taste the same every night. Throw all that in a pot, stew it for a while, and you'll have a dinner that's as good as what you might make at home.

Remember that "dry" is the operative word for backpacking food. Peanut butter is delicious, but it's a wet food, so it's heavy. (Ann Marie often brings a small jar of peanut butter anyway. It's a trade-off she's willing to live with.) Rice is a great choice for backpacking, but if you buy pre-cooked rice, it is wet food—meaning that it has water in it. Carry parboiled rice and you save a lot of weight. And it cooks quickly, too.

Weight isn't the only consideration; the amount of volume or space the food takes up in your pack also matters. Sometimes this can be fixed by removing packaging. Take a freeze-dried cup-of-noodles out of its package and put it in a Ziploc, and you just saved a ton of room in your pack.

If you look in the soup, pasta, and rice aisle of your favorite grocery store, you'll find many dried foods that are suitable for backpacking: microwaveable cups of freeze-dried mashed potatoes, quinoa, couscous, black beans, and so on. Don't carry these items in the cups that they are sold in. Empty out the contents into a Ziploc bag to save space and weight, then cook them up in a pot over your camp stove.

Grocery stories that have bulk foods sections are a bonanza for backpackers. Various kinds of beans are sold in dehydrated and flaked forms, so they easily rehydrate with hot water. Grains and pastas like couscous and orzo can be bought cheaply by the pound. They soak up a lot of water when cooked, so they're lightweight.

Ann Marie's food packing checklist includes the following for breakfast: oatmeal, raisins, nuts, Starbucks VIA instant coffee, and hot chocolate mix. For lunch, which usually takes place on the trail somewhere, she'll have crackers or tortillas, peanut butter, tuna packed in foil pouches, turkey jerky, and/or some trail mix or a trail bar. For dinner, she'll make a soup or a stew with brown rice or quinoa or couscous and whatever other ingredients she has. Or if she's too worn out to think about cooking, she'll "cheat" and have a bag of freeze-dried lasagna.

It's pretty easy to dry home-cooked sauces like marinara and pesto and bring them with you. (Just make sure they don't have meat in them; if you want meat in your meal, add dried jerky or foil packages of salmon, chicken, or tuna separately when you cook at camp.) A home dehydrator is a great tool, but you can do a lot with your own oven. Take a cookie sheet, spray with a little oil, and cover evenly with any sauce you've made. Turn on your oven to 175 degrees, crack the door open to let out moisture, and let it run for about ten hours. When the sauce is done, it will have a fruit-roll consistency. Cut it into small squares for easier transport. When you're in camp, just add the squares of sauce to boiling water.

Cooking Gear

We discussed stove and cooking needs in Chapter 4: Gear That Matters, but if you skipped that section, just remember that it's possible to do an entire trip with one pot, one cup for tea or coffee, and a spork. If you want to be a little more civilized, you can bring a folding bowl or plate so you don't have to eat out of the pot. This also allows you to start boiling more water for tea or a second course while you're eating the first course.

If you're obsessed with going ultralight, you can also forgo the stove. We would never do this; we're just saying that you can. Truthfully, we would give up sex and our retirement savings before giving up hot food and especially hot coffee. Some ultralight backpackers rehydrate their food in cold water and eat it that way. It's doable; it's just not as satisfying as a warm meal. And it takes a little planning: You pour dried couscous into a cup in the morning, add cold water, and it will be ready to eat by lunch.

6
Dealing with Critters

Bears

Holding nearly mythical status in the American psyche, bears are the animal icon of America's wilderness. Almost every national park visitor hopes to see a bear, but that hope is often mixed with trepidation. We love bears, but we also fear bears.

Any time a bear attacks a human, a flurry of media attention amplifies the horror. But let's put these rare events in perspective: in all of America's national parks, you are far more likely to be injured by a bison than by a bear. (And most national parks don't even have bison.)

More than three million people visit Yellowstone National Park every year, and yet, on average, only one of them gets injured by a bear. Four million people visit Yosemite National Park every year, yet no one in that park has been killed or seriously injured by a black bear (although there's been plenty of bear-caused damage to cars and buildings).

Of all US national parks, Glacier National Park has seen the highest number of deaths from bear attacks—but that's a total of ten people spread out over more than a century. Only three of those fatalities were hikers. Most recently, in June 2016, a mountain biker was killed by a grizzly just outside the entrance to Glacier National Park. In a

typical year, Glacier sees two million visitors and one or two bear-related injuries each year.

Want more bear statistics? In the United States, you are fifty times more likely to be killed by lightning or bee stings than bears. You are ten times more likely to be killed by a dog.

That said, bear attacks do occur, and are more common in some parts of the country than others. Grizzly bears are generally much more aggressive than black bears, but black bears, too, have attacked people. It's extremely rare, but it happens.

Know Your Bears

There are two types of bears in the United States—black and grizzly. About half of the fifty states have at least one kind of bear, and a few states have both. Black bears are deceptively named; not all black bears are black. Their fur color ranges from black to light brown to blonde. This type of bear is common throughout the eastern states, all along the West Coast, in the Rocky Mountains, and in parts of

Alaska. Black bears are also found in a few small areas in New Mexico and the Southwest, and in Georgia and other parts of the Southeast.

Black bears will usually try to avoid humans as much as possible; however, many have learned to patrol neighborhoods, parks, and campgrounds where human food and trash is readily available. In Yosemite National Park and Sequoia National Park, black bears frequently break into cars and buildings to obtain human food, but they tend to be fairly shy around people. Bear-caused break-ins have reduced substantially in the last fifteen years due to a strong public education campaign in these parks, but even so, if you leave a candy bar in your glove box, you may have your car windows broken, your seats clawed, and your door frames bent into odd angles.

Black bears in Great Smoky Mountains National Park seem to be more aggressive than their California cousins. In recent years, there have been increasing numbers of car break-ins and a few attacks on humans.

The majestic grizzly bear is found in a much smaller range than the black bear. Their numbers are greatest in Alaska, but they also are found in northwestern Montana, northern Utah, and a small section of northwest Washington. Grizzlies and brown bears are the exact same species; people in Alaska and Canada call grizzlies by the term "brown bear." Grizzlies tend to be much more aggressive than black bears, especially when a mother grizzly believes she must defend her cubs.

Staying Out of Bear's Way

A large percentage of grizzly attacks on hikers have occurred because a hiker surprised a bear. Grizzlies do not like surprises. In Glacier and Yellowstone, hikers are told to shout, "Hey bear!" and clap their hands loudly every few minutes, especially when following trails where visibility is limited—that is, in densely forested terrain or when coming around a blind curve. Solo hikers run the greatest risk of bear attacks because they often tromp along, lost in their own thoughts, hardly making a sound. It's easy for a solo hiker to accidentally startle a bear. People who hike in pairs or groups usually talk as they walk, and their noisy chatter gives bears a warning and a chance to fade back into the forest.

Wearing bells to ward off bears is nearly useless. The noise generated by bells doesn't carry well, especially in windy conditions or near fast-moving streams. Shouting and clapping sounds carry better.

Bear Spray

Park rangers in grizzly country will tell you to carry bear spray when you hike or backpack, but they'll also tell you not to rely on it. The best way to stay safe from bears is to avoid them (remember, be noisy).

In the rare event that an aggressive bear—black or grizzly—approaches you, you can protect yourself by spraying him or her in the face with capsaicin repellent. Capsaicin, derived from hot peppers, is sold commercially as Dog Shield and Halt! Dog Repellent. Mail carriers and meter readers use it to repel dogs, and it works just as well on black bears. A more concentrated version of capsaicin spray, which is carried by rangers in Glacier and Yellowstone, is sold under the name Counter Assault. Containing 2 percent capsaicin, this is the most potent formula permitted by the Environmental Protection Agency. Other popular bear sprays include Guard Alaska and Frontiersman. The key for making bear spray truly effective is not to bury it in your pack. Wear the spray canister on your belt or hip so you can easily grab it if you need it.

In order to work, the capsaicin spray must sting the bear's eyes, so it's critical to aim the spray at the bear's face. Many factors can influence the spray's effectiveness, including your distance from the bear, the direction of the wind, how wet the weather is, and even the spray's shelf life. (Check the expiration date.)

Protecting Your Food from Bears

Whether it's a black bear or a grizzly, every bear loves snacks. The average black bear has to eat as much as 30,000 calories a day, and since its natural diet is made up of berries, fruits, plants, fish, insects, and grubs, the high-calorie food that humans eat is very appealing to them. One bag of potato chips is worth a whole day's worth of digging for roots.

Any time you see a bear, it's almost a given that it's looking for food. Seeing bears foraging for natural food in the wild—digging up roots in a meadow or gorging on berries in the forest—is a fantastic experience. Unfortunately, bears have become specialists in the human-food-raiding business. It's hard to find a backpacker who doesn't have a story about bears stealing food.

Even day-hikers will sometimes have their food swiped, especially if they aren't paying attention. Some years ago, Ann Marie went for a long hike and then stopped to cool off her feet in a mountain stream. A young bear came along, grabbed her day-pack, and ran off with it in his mouth—while she was standing up to her knees in the creek about eight feet away. Fortunately the pack's main compartment was open, and as the bear ran, the contents fell out. The bear left Ann Marie's first-aid supplies, whistle, fleece jacket, and headlamp lying on the ground, but he scooped up the tuna fish sandwich and oatmeal cookie and disappeared into the forest.

Lesson learned: be absolutely certain that you make your food inaccessible to bears. In the backcountry, the best way to do this is to store your food in a bear-resistant food canister, a hard-sided, secure-locking plastic container that typically holds about three to five days' worth of food.

Bear-Resistant Canisters, or Bear Cans

Bear-resistant canisters are now required equipment for backpackers in many national parks, including Yosemite, Sequoia and Kings Canyon, Grand Teton, Rocky Mountain, North Cascades, Olympic, Denali, Glacier Bay, and Gates of the Arctic.

In New York's Adirondack Mountains, bear canisters are required in the High Peaks Wilderness Area. In California, most areas of Inyo National Forest, the Ansel Adams Wilderness, and the John Muir Wilderness also require hikers to carry bear canisters.

Some wilderness areas have gone a step further and constructed food-storage contraptions at popular backcountry campsites. Mount Rainier and Glacier National Park have metal food lockers or bear

Bear canisters come in a variety of shapes, sizes, and weights.

poles at major backpacking destinations. Sequoia National Park has installed food lockers at several backcountry locations. Great Smoky Mountains National Park has food-hanging cables.

Most parks that require bear canisters will rent them very cheaply to backpackers. In Yosemite, rental rates are only $5 for an entire week as long as you return the canister when you're finished. If you backpack often in bear country, you can buy your own bear canister at major outdoors stores. Expect to pay about $50 to $80 for most canisters that weigh just shy of three pounds, but if you must save weight, you can splurge on a $250-and-up carbon fiber Bearikade canister. This high-tech wonder is made by a trio of aerospace engineers at a California company called Wild Ideas. Through their website, you can rent a Bearikade for a few bucks a day and try it out before plunking down the big bucks to own one. Their "weekender"-sized canister weighs just under two pounds, so that's a significant one-pound savings.

Why do bear canisters work? Bears, like dogs, have incredibly skilled noses. They smell a lot better than backpackers do (yes, you can read that two different ways). In fact, most bears have a sense of smell that's at least 100 times more powerful than a dog's. No matter how hard you try to hide the bag of Cheez-Its you're hording for Day 4 of your trip, a bear can smell it from a quarter-mile away. With a bear canister, all that cheesy goodness is locked away in a vault that a bear can't open.

When you're in camp, pack your canister with anything that's scented—not just food but also trash, toothpaste, sunscreen, lip balm, etc. All of that stuff smells delicious to a bear. Then place your canister at least 100 feet (thirty paces) away from your campsite. Some people paint their canister with a splash of fluorescent paint so it is easier to locate. A bear may find your canister and roll it around, maybe beat on it a little, but after a while, he or she will give up. Don't put the canister next to a lake where it may wind up floating, or anywhere else that's hard to get to after a bear plays with it for a while.

Canisters are great for protecting food from bears, but plenty of backpackers complain about them because they're heavy. Most canisters weigh in around 2.7 pounds, which might be as much as 10 percent of your entire packload. In addition to being heavy, they're also bulky. Carry it in the center of your pack, close to your back, so the weight is centered.

One more downside: some hikers have trouble finding ways to fit all their food into a bear canister. Sorry, you may have to smash that bag of Cheez-Its to make it fit.

Not All Canisters Are Equal

Also, not all commercial bear canisters are created equal. Just because a manufacturer says its canister is bear-resistant doesn't mean the canister can stop every bear from breaking into it. Most wilderness areas requiring canisters specify which types are "approved" for use, which means they will stand up to the strength and cleverness of that park's bears.

Kerri Stevenson and her husband, Derek De Oliveira, learned the hard way about the variations in bear canisters while hiking the

211-mile John Muir Trail through the Sierra Nevada Mountains. Technically a section of the much longer Pacific Crest Trail, the John Muir Trail is known for its beautiful alpine lakes, granite cliffs, and spectacular vistas from 13,000-foot peaks. It's also known for hungry bears.

In 2012, Kerri and Derek traveled from their home in Canada to Yosemite National Park, where the John Muir Trail begins. Since they were both experienced backpackers, they had prepared well for their two-week trip. Their packs contained ultralight camping gear, emergency supplies, and two different types of bear canisters filled with toiletries and all of the food needed for the trip.

On the first day, they trekked through the mountain landscape that had inspired Ansel Adam's famous photographs. The nature-loving couple took their time, relishing the scenery as they hiked to 9,926-foot Clouds Rest, their camping destination for the first night.

"We walked in to our campsite and there was a little bear cub, lying horizontal in a tree," Kerri says. "I stopped, looked at Derek and said, 'It's time to turn around and leave.'"

Kerri feared that the cub's mother was close by—not a good scenario. But her husband insisted that they stay the night. "It's sunset," he told her, "and we aren't going to out-walk a bear."

The sun was already sinking, so Kerri agreed to stay, and the couple set up their tent as far as possible from the lounging cub. A park ranger, who also happened to be camping at Clouds Rest, strolled over to their camp to warn them about bears. "There's been a very active mom and her two cubs in the area," the ranger informed the couple. "They have gotten food every single night."

Kerri and Derek hastily made dinner and placed all their leftover garbage and scraps in their two bear canisters. One was a Bearikade, which is a cylindrical canister; the other an Ursack, a lightweight Kevlar bag. Both models were advertised as bear-resistant. Before crawling into her sleeping bag, Kerri placed both canisters outside the tent on the far fringes of the campsite. There was no way she was going to have them anywhere near her body.

"Sure enough, in the dark, in the middle of the night, I heard a 'grunt, grunt, grunt' outside of our tent," Kerri says. "Derek was fast asleep and didn't have a clue what was going on. My heart was going through my chest."

Instead of shooing away the bear, Kerri decided to play dead. "I was scared to death. I didn't want to make noise. I decided to pretend like I wasn't there and hope the bear would just go away."

The bear didn't go away. It crashed around the campsite for nearly an hour, preoccupied with the enticing scent emanating from the couple's bear canisters.

When morning came, Kerri and Derek left their tent to investigate the damage. "We found the Bearikade," Kerri recalls. "The bear had pushed it a long way from where it was stashed, but it survived really well. The canister had scratches all over it but no dents."

The Ursack, on the other hand, didn't fare well. Secured by a rope system that pulls from the top, "the bear hadn't gotten the knots undone but had eventually just gnawed through the Kevlar bag," Kerri says. "The Ursack was initially white, but when we found it, it was completely covered in blood from the bear's mouth. The bear ate everything in the Ursack, even the toothpaste and sunscreen."

The couple gathered the tattered Ursack and trashed remains of their food and stuffed them into the Bearikade, then debated what to do next. The bear had decimated half of their food and toiletries. Now they didn't have enough supplies to finish the two-week trip. They decided to hike to Tuolumne Meadows, seventeen miles away, to purchase more food and dispose of the bloody Ursack.

"Normally I never would have hiked seventeen miles on the second day with so much weight on my back," Kerri explains. "But we had all this garbage from the bears and we were down a canister. I didn't want to camp another night with the garbage and scented items not secured."

"So we hiked out and went to the ranger station," she says. The couple learned that Ursack was not one of Yosemite's "approved" bear canisters—and apparently with good reason. They rented one of the park's canisters, restocked their supplies, and headed back to the John Muir Trail.

"From then on, we were really careful to make sure that every scented item and snack was in those bear canisters, and all of our items were secured," Kerri notes. The couple had a bear-free trip for the next sixteen days.

The Food Hang

If you're backpacking in an area where bear canisters are NOT required, or where bears aren't as bold as they are in many national parks, you can substitute a food hang for a bear canister, but understand that this system is not as foolproof (or bear-proof). To make a food hang, you place your food in a canvas or nylon bag, tie it up tightly, then suspend it from a rope in midair, usually ten feet from the trunk of a tree and twenty feet off the ground.

The food hang is most easily accomplished by tying a rock to a long length of parachute cord or rope, then throwing it over a sturdy tree limb that's at least twenty feet high. (Make sure to hold on to the other end of the rope!) Next, tie your food bag to your end of the rope. Now you have a rock on one side of the limb and your food bag on the other. Hoist the food bag into the air by pulling down on the rock side of the rope. When you are satisfied with the position of the food bag, tie off the rock end of the rope to another tree.

Voilà. You have mastered the food hang. Bears in a three-mile radius around your camp are laughing their butts off. About an hour after dark, they'll come by to snap that cord with their claws and feast on your Cheez-Its. Or they'll send their small cubs up the tree and out on the limb to chew that cord to bits. It's piñata time!

A counterbalance food hang is somewhat more effective than a traditional food hang (emphasis on the word "somewhat"). With the counterbalance method, you divide your food into two bags of approximately equal size and weight and throw one of them over a twenty-foot-high tree limb. Position the bags so they are both about ten feet off the ground, and tie a section of nearly invisible fishing line to one bag so you can retrieve your food when you want it.

Whichever type of hang you use, be forewarned that if you weren't a quarterback on your high school football team, it may take

A hiker prepares to hang her food bag from a tree limb.

a couple of throws to get that rock (or food bag) slung over a twenty-foot-high limb. Both Terra and Ann Marie have been accused of throwing like girls. But that's probably because we are girls.

163

A final thought about bear-proofing your camping food: once a bear gets his mitts on your food, he considers it his. There is nothing you can do. If this happens to you one time, you will discover a new appreciation for bear-resistant canisters.

Bears and Your Vehicle

While we're discussing bears and food, it's worth mentioning proper trailhead protocol, too. If you're backpacking or hiking in any area where you need to protect food from bears, you should also protect your parked vehicle from bears. Never leave food or any scented items—sunscreen, lip balm, insect repellent—in your vehicle. In many national parks, you may get a ticket from a ranger for tempting the bears, or worse yet, you may have your car windows smashed in by a bear.

Guess what type of car gets broken into by Yosemite National Park bears more than any other? Wouldn't you know it, it's the mini-van. Little kids are frequent passengers in mini-vans, and little kids leave Cheerios and cookie crumbs and gummy bears and all kinds of yummy-smelling stuff underneath the car seats. Take your mini-van to the car wash for a detailing before you visit a bear-infested area.

Of course, not all bears are carjackers. Yosemite's black bears are notorious for breaking into cars, but just 100 miles north in the Lake Tahoe area, the black bears leave cars alone and break into houses and garages instead. There's a bear lounging underneath Ann Marie's back deck as she writes this. He may be hoping she'll pull a warm cherry pie from the oven and then drive off to run an errand. Dream on, Mr. Bear.

How Not to Keep Your Food Safe from Bears

When backpacking started to gain popularity in the 1960s and 1970s, many hikers believed that sleeping right next to their food was the best way to keep it safe. (Sounds dumb, we know. But it seemed like a good idea at the time.) Bears eventually smartened up to that routine and grew brave enough to walk into people's camp-sites and steal their stashes. Of course the bears told their cubs and their cubs' cubs about it. And that's why today's backpackers have to carry 2.7-pound bear canisters.

Kip Myers was one of those 1960s backpackers, and he remembers a Sierra trip when a bear outsmarted him and three of his UC Berkeley college buddies.

"Like typical college kids, we left late in the day and drove to the mountains, and when we got to our trailhead, it was dark. We decided to just sleep on the ground and start our backpacking trip in the morning," Kip remembers.

But one of Kip's friends was worried about leaving food in the car. He'd heard there were bears in the area and that they could totally destroy a car. The young men talked it over and agreed they didn't want to take the risk.

"So one of the guys got the bright idea that we should put our food in our backpacks, and then keep our backpacks really close to us. So we slept on the ground using our backpacks for pillows. We figured if the bears came, we would wake up and shoo them away," Kip says.

In the middle of the night, Kip woke up to a lot of noise. "I immediately checked my backpack, which was still under my head. There was this terrible crashing and banging noise maybe fifty feet away. I shined a flashlight over there and I saw that a bear was beating the crap out of an old stump.

"I couldn't figure out why the bear was smacking that stump so hard. There was a lot of noise, but none of the other guys woke up. Finally the bear stopped, and I went back to sleep. In the morning, I woke up again, and I looked around at my friends. I was still lying on my backpack, the guy on my left was lying on his, but Jerry, the guy on my right, was flat on the ground. I woke him up, and he was totally shocked when he realized his pack wasn't under his head."

Kip remembered the strange noises from the night before, and he led his friends over to the bear's stump. "Sure enough, there were the remains of Jerry's backpack. There were a few shreds of material and that was about it. Jerry was totally freaked out, of course. We never figured out how that bear did it, but somehow he managed to pull that pack out from under Jerry's head without waking him up."

Rodents, Large and Small

Backpackers go to a lot of trouble to protect their food from marauding bears, but in many places, a rodent will feast on your freeze-dried lasagna long before Ursa Major or Minor even catches a whiff. Bear-proofing your food is important—in fact, it's the law in many parks and wilderness areas—but the smaller creatures are often the most prolific camp robbers.

In some parts of the country, raccoons are the bandits. In other parts, it's squirrels and chipmunks. In the Sierra, one of the worst thieves is the yellow-bellied marmot, an otherwise charming member of the squirrel family that's about the size of a house cat. At the trail camp below the summit of 14,505-foot Mount Whitney, we

This yellow-bellied marmot would like to steal your snacks, and he's a crafty thief.

once watched a tent flopping and bulging and bobbing around on a perfectly windless day. It looked like it was filled with Japanese sumo wrestlers. We walked over to investigate and found a half-dozen marmots inside, beating each other up over whatever crumbs they could find. We shooed the marmots, but that tent was destroyed.

Even cute little chipmunks, Belding ground squirrels, and other adorable varmints can rob you of your food. Don't leave your day-pack or backpack lying around with food in it. If we leave our packs sit outside unattended for any period of time, we remove all food and open up every zipper compartment and pocket so that the critters are free to snoop around without gnawing through our expensive packs.

The same goes for day-hiking. Once, on an easy eight-mile day-hike, we walked about thirty feet away from our day-packs to do some fishing. Terra left her pack open but forgot that she had a trail bar inside. She returned to find a half-eaten trail bar and some tiny (but still identifiable) chipmunk pellets inside her pack. He ate, pooped, and scampered away.

On another occasion, we were hiking in Canada's Banff National Park when a twenty-something woman approached us, clearly unhappy. "Do you have any food you could share?" she asked. We pulled trail bars and beef jerky from our packs. As she scarfed them down, we noticed that she was hiking in flip-flops, and her pack looked pretty ragged. We were just about to ask what happened, when she explained: "I was backpacking last night and the porcupines got all my food. And they chewed up my backpack and leather boots."

Porcupines? We're Californians. Our state's porcupines are about the size of a large hamster, and we rarely see them unless our dogs sniff one out of its hiding place. Even then, we usually see only the creature's defensive spines poking out of our dogs' muzzles—not the animal itself, which usually disappears up the nearest tree.

The hungry woman told us more about how a family of porcu-pines had invaded her camp and ate everything they could find. We nodded sympathetically. As soon as she walked away, we burst out laughing. "Raided by porcupines? That's hilarious. There's no way they were porcupines."

Porcupines can use their sharp claws to shred your backpack.

About twenty minutes farther down the trail, we met up with a Canadian porcupine. To be more exact, he was a pig-sized critter that was covered in spines—just like a porcupine only much larger and more ornery than what we were used to. He blocked the trail and wouldn't get out of our way. Suddenly the woman's story seemed a whole lot more believable.

It turns out the porcupine is North America's second largest rodent, after the beaver, and yes, it likes to dine on leather and salty snacks. Its natural food is tree bark, but the porcupine is happy to eat whatever you've brought for backpacking food. And it will gnaw through your pack to get it. Porcupines think leather hiking boots are an epicurean delight.

The western subspecies of porcupine may be fairly small and stealthy, but in Canada and Alaska and the Northwest states, porcupines can wreak havoc. They've been known to eat canoe paddles, tools, and wooden campground shelters. They are attracted to almost any object that has been handled by humans because of the salt found in human sweat. They also like to eat glue, car hoses, and wiring.

Danger from Deer Mice: Hantavirus

In August 2012, a rash of alarming media reports told of death and serious illness among Yosemite National Park visitors, caused not by lightning or rockfall, but by deer mice. The culprit was an infection known as hantavirus pulmonary syndrome (HPS), a rare but serious disease caused by a virus that humans contract through contact with the urine, droppings, or saliva of deer mice.

Ten visitors who stayed one night or more in Yosemite in June and July 2012 contracted the disease, which causes severe flu-like symptoms. Three people died; the other seven recovered. Nine of the ten spent at least one night in Curry Village's "signature tent cabins," which had insulated walls. The insulation may have attracted a larger-than-normal population of deer mice, who built warm, cozy nests in the walls. (After the outbreak, these cabins were demolished.)

Deer mice are found throughout the United States, and it is estimated that 12 percent of American deer mice carry hantavirus. The disease can also be carried by the cotton rat, rice rat, and white-footed mouse. Since HPS was first identified as a disease in 1993, approximately 600 cases have been confirmed in the United States. About thirty Americans come down with hantavirus annually. Symptoms include fever, muscle aches, cough, dizziness, nausea, vomiting, and diarrhea. In other words, it seems like a bad flu. But as the disease progresses, it leads to severe difficulty in breathing. About half the people who contract it will die. There is no cure.

Why such a concentrated outbreak of HPS occurred in a small area of Yosemite in a short time remains a mystery. But now the Park Service urges visitors to avoid touching live or dead rodents or disturbing rodent burrows, dens, or nests. If you're camping, keep your food and water in tightly sealed containers to protect it from mice. If you leave your bag of trail mix on a rock for two minutes and come back to find chew marks in the bag, don't eat it. Also take care not to inhale dust that carries traces of rodent excrement. People have caught the virus from sweeping out dusty cabins, trail shelters, and barns.

Mountain Lions

The magnificent mountain lion used to roam in all fifty of the United States, but today the big cat is found mostly in fourteen western states. Florida also has a small population, which residents call the Florida panther, but it's the same species—*Puma concolor*. (Their Latin name means their coat is one uniform color, tan.) Other common names include cougar, puma, and catamount. Thriving in deserts, along the coast, on arid hillsides, and in pine forests and scrub and oak woodlands, these big felines are versatile creatures. They can live from sea level to high mountain summits. Anywhere in the West where deer are prevalent, mountain lions are usually nearby.

Most people will never see a mountain lion, but the cat is incredibly easy to identify by its long and heavy tail. Most mountain lions measure between six and eight feet long from nose to tail tip, but almost two-thirds of that is tail. The cats typically weigh between 100 and 180 pounds (the females are smaller). The only other wildcat in America is the bobcat, and it would take about four bobcats to fill the space of a mountain lion.

Mountain lions are generally solitary and elusive creatures who want no interaction with people. Human encounters with mountain lions are rare, and the risk of an attack is infinitely small. But when the big cats show themselves, they receive a lot of media attention. A handful of mountain lion attacks on hikers in California, Colorado, New Mexico, and Arizona in the last thirty years have been widely publicized. Still, the vast majority of hikers never see a mountain lion, and those who do usually report that the cat vanished into the brush at the first sign of nearby humans.

If you do encounter a mountain lion, do not run away. If you run, the cat will think you're prey, and he or she will try to catch you. Mountain lions can run at speeds of up to fifty miles per hour, so running is useless. Instead, act like the hunter, not the hunted. Do not turn your back on the cat. Stand tall and make yourself bigger by waving your arms. Yell and shout. If you have children with you, pick them up off the ground, but try to do it without crouching down or leaning over. (Crouching makes you appear smaller and less aggressive, more like prey.) If you must move, back away slowly and deliberately, always retaining your aggressive pose and continuing to speak loudly. Even after attacking, lions have been successfully fought off by adult hikers and even children who used rocks and sticks to defend themselves.

Hello Kitty

In the summer of 1995, John Kleinfelter was a fisheries biologist working with the California Fish and Game Department to monitor golden trout populations in the Sierra Nevada Mountains. John and his work colleagues spent that summer wandering through mountain watersheds, often camping in the wilderness for weeks at a time.

During one expedition, the biologists camped on Camelback Ridge, a rocky crest high above the shimmering waters where they worked. It was an ideal location, close to the scientists' study area but high above the trees, which protected the camp from large animals.

"One of the reasons we wanted to camp there was because the bears would be less likely to find us," John says.

John and his partner Christy worked together, hiking down from the ridge each day and exploring the basins below. With few trails in the area, the colleagues often had to trek through dense scrub and underbrush, bushwhacking to hidden pools where the brightly colored golden trout gathered.

One afternoon, as John and Christy trudged upstream through icy, knee-deep water, they came across a series of impassable cascades, forcing them to follow a small trail that meandered beside the creek instead.

"As we were walking on that trail, we looked down and saw mountain lion tracks," John says. "It was funny because the name of the creek we were on was Lion Creek."

The biologists examined the paw prints closely. "If you know what you're looking for, you can tell mountain lion tracks apart from a dog, coyote, or any other animal with big paws," John says. Mountain lions have a distinctive "M"-shaped pad with three lobes on the rear of the heel. Their claw marks do not show in the track. John and Christy were interested by the tracks, but not particularly alarmed.

"We'd had a really long day. We were wet from stepping in the creek, tired, and hungry," John says. "Besides, it was hard to say if the mountain lion was stalking us, or if it was just walking up the trail."

In the fading light, the biologists headed back toward camp. The last rays of sunlight barely illuminated the overgrown forest, making it difficult for them to see the trail. They kept moving by the light of their headlamps. John loped ahead, but Christy's pace slowed, and the distance between the pair lengthened.

"We were starting to get separated from each other," John says. He sat and waited for his colleague to catch up. Looking down on the trail below, all he could see he was Christy's headlamp, a small bobbing light in the darkness. "Are you coming?" he called into the night. "Are you okay?"

Christy answered, her voice thin and gasping. "Yes. I'm almost there." She was exhausted, so John walked with her the rest of the way.

"When we got back to camp, all the other biologists were already there," John says. Their campfire dinner sizzled in a skillet and everyone was playing card games. John retreated to his tent, anxious to shed his wet shoes and socks. As he crawled inside, he heard a loud commotion.

"Everybody was shouting and yelling. Two mountain lions had come in and crouched down on the edge of our camp." John knew immediately that he should have paid more attention to those mountain lion tracks. "The cats had followed Christy and me all the way back to camp."

John's boss called out, "I'm going to shoot my gun off to try to scare them away," and there was a loud crack as a bullet blasted into the night sky.

"I was pulling off my shoes and socks, and I heard something crash through the brush," John says. "As I lifted my head to see what was going on, I saw the tails of two lions jumping over my tent."

The noise scared off the big cats, but nobody in camp slept very well that night. John says it was a wildlife lesson he will never forget. From that moment forward, no matter how badly he wanted to reach a destination, he always stayed close to his hiking companion.

"Don't leave your partner behind," he advises. "Hike together when you're in mountain lion territory, especially at night. You never know what might be out there."

Insects: Avoiding Bites and Itches

Mosquitoes and Other Nuisances

There's not much that can deter Terra from having fun in the outdoors. Rain? No problem—she puts on her rain gear and goes fishing. Steep hills? The tougher the grade, the better the payoff, she says. July snowstorm? It's all part of the mountain adventure. Mosquitoes? Oh crap. Now she wants to go home.

On our backpacking trips, we've been known to eat our meals inside the tent just to get a break from the mosquitoes. We've foregone our usual rest stops and even flat-out sprinted the last few miles to our cars—with full packs on our backs—just to avoid another hour of swatting at our arms and legs. On rare occasions when we've been hiking through a wet meadow with a cloud of mosquitoes buzzing around our eyes and ears, we've wished we could be anywhere else on earth—even at our jobs.

But when we feel this way, we try to remember the hiker's motto: *God put mosquitoes in the mountains so that we would know we are not yet in heaven.* And then we put bug nets over our hats and hike onward.

Insect Repellents

In some parts of the country at certain times of the year, insect repellent is an absolute must for traveling in the outdoors. But in other places, mosquitos have a relatively short season, and you can time your trips to avoid the worst of the bugs. We've learned that by August and September, the Sierra is mostly mosquito-free, so that's our favorite time to backpack. The best wildflower months—June and July—are notoriously buggy, so we slather on the repellent then, and we often do more day-hiking in those months and less backpacking.

What repellent works best? Every hiker has an opinion. In the middle of a major mosquito hatch, it often seems like nothing works except covering your entire body in mosquito netting (or taking cover in your tent).

Many types of insect repellent have an ingredient called DEET, which is extremely effective but also quite toxic. Pregnant women and small children definitely should not use repellent with high levels of DEET, and it's not recommended for adults, either. It can damage plastic, rubber, and vinyl—a car dashboard can melt from spilled DEET—so it's hard to imagine that it's good for your skin.

Other types of repellents are made of natural substances, such as lemon eucalyptus oil or citronella. We are fond of a repellent called

During the peak of a mosquito hatch, taking cover in your tent may be the only way to escape the bugs.

Natrapel, which is DEET-free and available in various-sized spray bottles. It contains a 20 percent picaridin formula, which is a synthetic compound recommended by the Centers for Disease Control and World Health Organization for insect bite protection. It repels insects, ticks, and chiggers.

Besides repellent, we also carry lightweight mosquito head nets that drape over our hats. They lessen the clear view of the beautiful mountain scenery, but at least they keep the maddening buzzing away from eyes, ears, and noses. Unfortunately, if you want to drink water or eat a snack, you have to lift the netting up over your mouth—which can let in mosquitoes.

It's also a smart idea to wear only light-colored clothing when in mosquito country. Most studies show that given a choice, mosquitoes will go for the hiker in the navy blue T-shirt instead of the hiker in the off-white T-shirt.

Unless you're eating or drinking, a mosquito net over a baseball cap will keep the bugs off your face.

Our only other mosquito advice is to avoid them. Stay away from the terrain that bugs prefer, which includes grassy areas like meadows, deeply shaded areas like forests, and watery places, especially where the water isn't moving (fast-moving creeks are usually safe, but ponds and lakes are mosquito nurseries). If you're looking for a place to get away from insects, find a spot that is high, dry, rocky, and exposed to the wind. Mosquitoes almost always disappear when it's windy. Amen to that.

Some Minnesota hiking friends swear by clothing treated with the insecticide permethrin (and in Minnesota, everybody has an honorary PhD in mosquitoes). You can buy permethrin and apply it to your own clothes. Some manufacturers like ExOfficio sell clothing that is pre-treated with it, but it does wash out after several rounds in the laundry.

Mother Nature provides plenty more biting bugs—black flies, no-see-ums, horse flies, etc.—but most of our mosquito advice applies to those other annoying creatures, too.

Ticks

Flying insects aren't the only entomological annoyances out there. Ticks can be troublesome, too, especially at lower elevations. In the United States, there are nearly 100 varieties of ticks, and many are harmless. But some carry Lyme disease or Rocky Mountain spotted fever. These diseases can take a terrible toll on your health.

Some tick bites cause a sharp sting that will get your attention. Other times, ticks will bite without you noticing. If you've been in the outdoors, and then a few days or a week later start to experience flu-like symptoms like headaches, fever, muscle soreness, neck stiffness, or nausea, see a doctor immediately. Tell the doctor you are concerned about possible exposure to ticks.

Rocky Mountain spotted fever can be fatal in the first eight days of symptoms, so what matters most is getting to a doctor immediately after symptoms develop. In addition to the flu-like symptoms, many victims of Rocky Mountain spotted fever will develop a spotted rash on their limbs, hands, and feet.

Lyme disease victims will also experience flu-like symptoms. They may also have a telltale red rash—like a round bulls-eye mark—near the tick bite, which appears a week to three weeks after the bite. Caught in its early stages, Lyme disease is easily treated with antibiotics, but left untreated, it can be severely debilitating. As with Rocky Mountain spotted fever, you need to seek medical attention immediately.

The best way to remove a tick is by grasping it as close to your skin as possible, then pulling it gently and slowly straight up and out, without twisting or jerking it. Tweezers work well for the job, and many Swiss Army knives include tweezers. It's not uncommon for the tick's head to remain inside your skin after you've removed its body. This can lead to an infection, so it's important to work carefully and slowly to remove all parts of the tick, then clean and disinfect the wound.

After the tick is removed, wash the bite site with soap and water, rubbing alcohol, iodine, or whatever you have in your first-aid kit. Apply a triple antibiotic ointment and keep the wound covered with a Band-Aid.

You may have heard a lot of folk remedies for removing ticks—smothering them with Vaseline, dousing them with alcohol, burning them with a match, and so on—but the tweezer is the only way to go.

Prevention is the best remedy for ticks: Wear long pants and long sleeves when you hike in tick-infested areas, and tuck your pant legs into your socks. The same insect repellent that you'd wear for mosquitoes will also repel ticks, so use it liberally on your clothing.

Always check yourself thoroughly when you leave the trail, looking carefully for anything that might be crawling on you. Wearing light-colored clothing makes it easier to see ticks. Check your clothes thoroughly, and also your skin underneath. A good friend can be a useful assistant in this endeavor.

And if your dog hikes with you, make sure your dog is free of ticks before you let him or her into your house. Terra has found ticks in her house several days after she hiked in tick country. Her best guess is that the tick was hitching a ride on her dog all that time and finally decided to let go.

Insects that Sting: Bees, Wasps, Scorpions, and More

When Ann Marie was about six years old, she went on a family vacation to the Florida Everglades. As she and her family wandered along a boardwalk trail through the rainforest, she put her hand on a tree trunk—only it wasn't a tree trunk, it was a wasp's nest. While her sisters and parents ran away screaming, she was stung more than twenty times. (It was a perilous beginning to a long love affair with nature and the outdoors.)

About thirty years later, she was reminded of this event on a backpacking trip in the Grand Canyon. She woke up in the morning and started to pull on her boots, but just as she started to cram in her toes, she spotted a giant scorpion sleeping inside.

The moral of her two stories: watch where you put your hands and feet.

If you're stung by a bee, wasp, or scorpion, a few basic first-aid items can help: oral antihistamines like Benadryl or Dimetane, topical steroids like Cortaid, or local anesthetics like Benzocaine. And for heaven's sake, if you know you're allergic to bee or wasp stings, make sure you have your medication with you—even on a day-hike, and even in places where you don't expect to see bees or wasps. An epinephrine injection can save your life when you are miles from the nearest hospital. Also, ask your health care provider about preventive injections that are now available for people who are allergic to many types of stings.

7
Weather and Elements

Hypothermia

In October of 1979, John Kleinfelter was an outdoorsy kid just out of high school, planning his first backpacking trip to Sequoia National Park. Although famous for its giant sequoia trees—the largest trees on earth by volume—the park also contains some of the Sierra Nevada's highest peaks and thousands of acres of pristine backcountry.

"It's a fantastic area with hundreds of miles of trails," John says. "I wanted to go farther up into the mountains and see more of what was up there."

John had hiked with his dad and camped with his high school backpacking club in Sequoia, but he had never executed a trip without adult supervision. He invited two of his friends to join him. The three buddies were all backpacking club members and itching to hike in the wilderness on their own.

"We had this idea that it would be a great adventure," John says. "We were fit, we were all athletes, and we were young and invincible."

They decided to tackle a trail out of Mineral King, a glacially carved valley cushioned by 12,000-foot peaks in southern Sequoia National Park. They would hike to Bullfrog Lakes, a pair of alpine tarns huddled at the base of a cirque, where they'd camp for one or two nights.

One problem: none of them had any backpacking gear. "We didn't even own a tent," John recalls, "and the whole idea of layering clothing was foreign to us."

It was early September, and the three friends thought it might be chilly at 10,000 feet, so they packed their heaviest parkas and jeans. They grabbed a couple pots and pans from their mothers' kitchens and borrowed a small two-man tent from a friend. They left the trailhead in the early afternoon, hiking six miles on a trail that meandered up to a 10,500-foot pass. At the top of the pass, they stopped and studied the terrain. From there, the trail went downhill for two miles before doubling back to Bullfrog Lakes. But they also saw a game trail, barely visible, that skirted along a ridge towards their destination.

"We decided to save time and traverse cross-country," John says. The three young men pranced across the ridgeline, easily making it to Bullfrog Lakes in under an hour. But when they arrived, they were surprised at how dark the sky had become. The weather was completely different than when they left the trailhead.

None of them had bothered to check the forecast before they left home. "Suddenly it was really cold and grey. Night was coming, so we decided to make camp. We didn't realize that a storm was approaching. It turns out this was one of those 'look-out-because-here-it-comes' first storms of the year."

After supper, the three friends crawled into their tiny two-man tent. The weather outside was eerily calm and the temperature was dropping. John's friends teased him when he chose to sleep in the middle for warmth.

"We were crammed into this tent like sardines," John remembers. "Little did we know that having a two-man tent with three people inside would probably save our lives."

Lulled by physical exhaustion, they quickly fell asleep, but a few hours later, they were jolted awake. Their flimsy tent shook violently as huge gusts of wind battered their camp. "The storm had come in, and it came with a vengeance. The tent poles were flapping like flags in the wind," John says.

"We looked outside, and it was a whiteout blizzard. Snow was blowing in all directions. We were in this little orange tent getting battered by a winter storm."

In the turbulence, the shock cords that held their tent erect were like pieces of string. The tent collapsed on top of them, but the men held up its sides with their bodies. "That tent was held up by sheer over-capacity," John says.

They lay awake, listening to the raging storm outside. "I remember my friend saying, 'Okay boys, the Hells Angels are coming down.' We didn't even have to ask what that meant because when the wind came howling down the ridge, it sounded like a hundred Harley Davidson motorcycles barreling toward us."

The friends were convinced they wouldn't survive the nightmarish storm. John remembers telling them: "I don't know if we are going to make it, but if we don't, I wouldn't want to be with anyone else but my best friends."

The hours slowly ticked by, and toward morning, the howling wind silenced. "We got out of our tent and there was snow everywhere, at least two feet," John says.

They looked up at the sky, and a small patch of brilliant blue peeked through the dark clouds like a benevolent angel peering down on them. They knew this was their chance to get out of there.

They broke down their tent, shook the snow off their gear, and started hiking. The snow grew deeper as they neared the game trail, and by the time they reached the ridge, they were wading through thigh-deep snowdrifts. It took three cold, miserable hours to cover the half-mile back to the main trail.

As they trudged, the friends shivered in their parkas and jeans. "I had on seven layers of clothing. Four layers under my wool shirt, a blue parka, and a rain jacket over that. But when I got to the top of the pass, I was still freezing cold," John recalls. "It must have been well below zero with the wind chill at 10,000 feet. At one point I took off my gloves and my fingers froze instantly."

The group kept moving to keep their bodies warm, slogging back downhill to the trailhead where their car was waiting to take them back to warmth and civilization.

Now, nearly four decades later, John owns a backcountry guide service. Clients pay him to lead them safely in and out of the wilderness. He says he still utilizes the big lesson he learned on that trip: There's no such thing as a surprise storm.

"Now, before every trip, I check the weather forecast. If it's a week-long trip, I check the extended forecast," he says. "Some people say I'm obsessed with checking the weather, but I always have a good idea of what's going to happen out there, and I'm prepared."

Weather in the mountains is notoriously unpredictable; even in July, you can't depend on warm days and balmy nights. The higher elevations of the Rocky Mountains and Sierra Nevada Mountains have recorded snow in every month of the year. Check the weather, know what Mother Nature is planning to throw at

In the mountains, pack along gear for almost any kind of weather, even on blue-sky summer days.

you, and you can alter your trip plans or at least pack along extra clothing and protective gear.

The penalty for not being prepared for cold or wet weather is hypothermia, and it's one of the biggest killers in the outdoors. Hypothermia occurs when your body loses heat faster than it can produce heat, lowering your body temperature below its normal 98.6 degrees Fahrenheit. If your body temperature goes down by just a couple of degrees, you are in serious danger. The science behind hypothermia is fairly simple: If your body's core temperature drops low enough, your vital organs can no longer function.

When you think of someone experiencing hypothermia, you might imagine a dramatic emergency like someone falling into an icy river, or a stormy night like the one John Kleinfelter endured. While situations like these can lead to hypothermia, so can more commonplace ones. Most hypothermia cases occur at temperatures in the forties or fifties, not below freezing. It often happens when the victim has gotten wet or is exhausted from physical exertion and/or lack of sleep.

Here's a classic example: Suzy goes on a day-hike to the top of a mountain peak on a warm summer afternoon. She feels hot on the sunny climb uphill, and she sweats a lot. When she reaches the summit, her clothes are drenched. It's very windy on the summit, and now, since it's late afternoon, the sun is much lower in the sky. Suzy starts to feel cold while on the summit, so she heads downhill, still wearing her wet, sweaty clothes and now hiking in the shade. She quickly realizes that she can't stop moving or she will be too cold. Even though she's tired and would like to stop for a snack and a rest, she keeps trucking along until her right foot trips over a rock. She twists her ankle and falls. Now she's on the ground, unable to move, and hypothermia starts to set in—even though just a few hours ago she was sweating from the heat.

Hypothermia's classic signs are the "umbles," —stumbles, mumbles, and fumbles. People experiencing the beginning stages of hypothermia may shiver violently or they may not shiver at all. They most likely will have trouble controlling their body movements and speech. They will walk and move sluggishly, and they may even try to lie down and sleep. Hypothermia comes on gradually and stealthily, so a person experiencing these symptoms may not recognize what's happening.

Search-and-rescue expert Chris Kozlowski says that hypothermia is particularly dangerous for solo hikers—they may not be thinking clearly enough to realize what's going on, and there's no one there to think for them.

"With the beginning stages, you lose fine motor control of your fingers, so it's hard to zip things up, to get things going. You will feel tired and not think clearly. Sometimes with mild hypothermia, you just sit down, you don't want to move," Chris says. "I had a friend who was wearing cotton while he was hiking. He got rained on and soaked and he just lay down on the trail. He couldn't get up. It didn't even occur to him to get up. It was just a full body shut down."

The best prevention for hypothermia is to be prepared for challenging weather conditions. Wet and/or cold weather is the leading cause, so check the forecast and then dress appropriately. Proper clothing choices can set you up to survive almost any weather conditions. Wear or carry multiple layers, even on beautiful sunny days. Leave cotton garments at home. If you sweat in a cotton T-shirt, you can kiss your body heat goodbye. Water conducts heat away from the body twenty-five times faster than air, so staying dry is critical. The best layers to wear next to your skin are made of silk, polyester, or polypropylene because they wick moisture and hold in body heat. For an outer layer, wear or carry a waterproof, wind-breaking jacket. Pack along a wool hat and gloves or mittens.

If you think your hiking partner is experiencing hypothermia, jump into action to get him or her warm and dry immediately. Remove any wet clothes and put on dry ones. Cover the person's head with a warm hat. Get the hypothermic person to eat some quick-energy food, even candy, and drink warm beverages—this helps the body produce heat. Do not give the person alcohol, as this encourages heat loss. If possible, put the person in a sleeping bag, or make a "hypothermia wrap." Wrap the person in as many sleeping

A waterproof jacket and a hat can be just enough insulation to keep you from going hypothermic.

bags as you have available, then wrap a tarp or a tent around the sleeping bags to further insulate them. This thermal burrito can help to bring the victim's temperature back up to normal.

Lost and Freezing Close to Home

What follows is a story about the bewilderment of being lost, and what it feels like to drop into the rabbit hole where nothing is where you think it should be. But that's not the worst part. It's also a story about the dangers of hypothermia. Getting lost is bad, but it won't kill you. Hypothermia can kill you.

Richard Platt was eighty-two years old when he got lost in the woods. Richard is not your typical octogenarian; he's an outdoorsman who has spent decades hiking, backpacking, and skiing in the West. He joined the Mount Hood Ski Patrol when he was seventeen years old. He worked as a Forest Service ranger in Sisters, Oregon.

185

He has aided in numerous search-and-rescue missions. His family calls him a "mountain goat."

In early June 2012, Richard and his wife, Shelley, went mushroom hunting in Payette National Forest, about a thirty-minute drive from their house near McCall, Idaho. They parked their vehicle at an old Forest Service guard station, then walked across the footbridge over Lake Fork Creek, which was roaring with spring runoff.

"The weather was warm and nice. We planned to be gone only an hour or so, as I had medications to take. I decided to leave my coat in the car and wore only a light flannel shirt and hiking pants," Richard narrates. Shelley walked in one direction; Richard walked the opposite way, eyes to the ground.

"My wife and I had hunted that area two or three years in a row, so we were pretty familiar with it. We didn't usually hunt for mushrooms close together. We'd split up to cover more ground."

Finding mushrooms requires slow walking and a close examination of the ground near your feet. To stay in touch, the Platts had a system of calling out to one another every few minutes.

"At some point I called out to my wife and didn't get a response. But I kept wandering around looking for mushrooms. I was sure that I was headed in her general direction," he says.

But he wasn't. Perhaps it was because he had been staring at the dirt, preoccupied with his mushroom search. Quite possibly the medication he was taking made him a little loopy, or maybe he just got lost in his thoughts. But somehow Richard, who was usually a top-notch navigator, had wandered away from, not toward, his wife.

He kept shouting. No response.

Richard wasn't sure exactly where he was, but he knew that his car was on the opposite side of the creek. He thought he might have walked far enough downstream that it made sense to keep going in that direction until he reached a shallow spot called Brown's Pond, where he figured he could safely ford, then walk upstream to his car. He spotted a high ridge nearby and decided to climb it to get his bearings.

"I started climbing, thinking I would top the ridge and get a good look around, then drop back down the other side. But it turned out to be much higher than I thought," he says. Heading uphill didn't seem productive, so he turned and hiked back down. At the bottom, Richard miscalculated his position.

"I'm not sure what happened next. The best I can reckon is that after I descended that ridge, I somehow started heading 180 degrees in the wrong direction," he recalls.

He kept wandering until he found a skid road, but then he miscalculated again: "I turned left when I should have turned right. I went to the end of the road and it ended in a logging landing. So then I retraced my steps in the other direction."

Richard was feeling tired from the extra wandering, but his mind was still sharp. "Even though I was lost, I felt very calm and rational. I kept stopping to draw maps in the dirt to help with my confusion. But my body was worn out. I had done some pretty serious hiking going up that ridge."

Still, he was confident he would soon find his way, so he kept moving. "I finally found the ford near Brown's Pond. I had been there before, and I recognized it. This was the first moment that I was sure where I was, but by now the sun had gone down and it was almost dark."

Richard considered fording across, but the snow fed creek was running about six feet deep and forty feet wide. "I knew it was too dangerous. I would just have to wait where I was."

Richard glanced at his watch, which had a compass, altimeter, and a light, and made an unhappy discovery. "It was crazy. On this day of all days, the battery had gone dead," he says. So he waited by the creek, hoping that by this late hour, his wife would have reported him missing and searchers would be out looking for him.

As night came on, the sky filled with clouds, and it started to rain. Since he was wearing only a light shirt and pants, Richard sought shelter under some pine trees. The air temperature was dropping, and Richard pulled out the only tool he had.

"I had this little keychain knife with a blade about an inch and a half long. I thought I would cut some little pine boughs and cover myself with them, like a blanket. But that little knife couldn't cut anything of decent size. I cut about twenty little boughs, and I tried lying down and putting them all over my chest, but they were too small. They just slid off," he says.

Richard had taken enough first-aid courses to know he was in danger of going hypothermic in the wet, cold night air.

"I started to shake, and it was quite different than shivering. I shook so badly that I actually chewed into my cheek. I hurt all over. Sometimes I could make the shaking stop for a minute or so, but then it would start up again."

Richard's only comfort was to try different positions to get some warmth in his body. He used a five-foot-long stick as a cane to help move his stiff, aching legs.

"There was a log near me. I would sit down on the log, then I would sit down on the ground and lean against the log, then I'd get up and lie down next to the log. The best position was sitting on the log and leaning forward with my arms across my chest. This fetal position seemed to preserve heat better than others."

With a black sky and no way to judge the time, Richard set his hopes on the coming of dawn. "Time seemed to pass awfully slowly. I tried to sleep but could not due to pain and cold. My thoughts were primarily on trying not to shake. My body was showing signs of real trouble."

Somehow, Richard made it to the morning. At first light, he started looking for a place where he could safely cross the creek. "I knew that another night like that would kill me," he recalls. "I had to get out of there."

He limped along the creek for an hour or so, but the high water was impassible, so he returned to where he had spent the night and made a new plan: He would rest a while, then hike back upstream, which he was now certain was the right way to go. "I was having trouble walking, but I thought that with time I could do it," he says. "I knew I had to do it."

But as Richard rested on a stump, his luck changed dramatically. Two search-and-rescue volunteers in a pickup truck spotted him from across the creek. There was a lot of shouting and commotion, and finally a boat was launched. Within a few minutes, Richard was surrounded by people who were covering him in blankets and giving him food and water.

Richard was taken to the hospital, but the doctors released him later that day, amazed by his physical and mental toughness. He'd suffered hypothermia, but his body withstood it. Later he learned that the air temperature had dropped to 45 degrees that night—cold enough to induce hypothermia in a hiker much younger than him.

"After I got out of the hospital, I just slept and slept. I can't tell you how tired I was. That was the worst night of my life," he says.

Richard Platt will be the first person to tell you that he was extremely lucky that night. Hypothermia is a sneaky predator, and if you're alone when it strikes, you're in serious danger. Although the event happened four years ago, Richard says he still feels sheepish about "being the woodsman who got lost." But he's grateful that his body was hardy enough to withstand hypothermia.

Richard's son John will be the second person to tell you that his father was lucky. John Platt, too, is an experienced outdoorsman. He's an expert hiker, climber, skier, and cyclist who once held a spot on the US Cycling Team. For the last four years, he's volunteered for Valley County Search and Rescue in Idaho, where he's witnessed some interesting hypothermia cases.

"Probably the worst case was the guy we found who had gone into end-stage hypothermia, which is the stage in which people take off all their clothes. When we found him, all he had on was a pair of Batman underwear. He'd been wandering barefoot off the trail for miles," he says.

End-stage hypothermia is uncommon, but it's a killer. Moderate hypothermia can also kill if not stopped in time. In fact, hypothermia is the third most common cause of death in the outdoors—after drowning and falls.

John Platt says that his father's uncontrollable shaking plus his difficulty walking and sluggish movements were classic hypothermia symptoms. "There's no question that it could have been a lot worse," he says.

And, like his dad, John also has a story about spending a cold night outdoors and unprepared.

The younger Platt's adventure occurred in Yosemite Valley, where he and a friend were rock climbing at Royal Arches. Like most climbers, they carried as little as possible with them. But their climb took longer than they anticipated, and they had to finish the last pitch in the dark. They still had to hike back down to their car in Yosemite Valley, and that meant a 1,500-foot elevation drop from the top of Royal Arches.

"The way off the top was to walk across an area known as the 'Death Slabs.' We had heard about the Death Slabs and we knew better than to try to go down them in the dark. We didn't have headlamps."

The men were going to have to spend the night right where they were. It had been a sunny, warm October day, so they wore only lightweight clothing. They had climbed with only one backpack, which had in it a water bottle and a couple of bars.

"We both knew what we were in for that night, so we said 'Okay, let's not be shy about this.' We laid our rope down on the ground to give us some insulation, and then we lay down together and started spooning. Basically, we made it through the night by cuddling."

The night air was so still that as the men lay on the granite, they could hear people going in and out of Yosemite's Ahwahnee Hotel, 1,500 feet below them. "We could actually hear them discussing what they had to eat for dinner," he says. "We wanted to lean over the side and yell, 'shut up!'"

"My friend was wearing shorts, so he had a lot of skin exposed. He kept shivering and keeping us both awake. We kept trying to figure out some way to cover his bare skin. I finally realized that I had a bandana, and I laid that over his legs. It was just enough insulation to help."

Just like with his father's story, things turned out okay for John Platt and his friend. "When dawn came, we made the long walk down, but we were like zombies. We'd had almost no sleep," John says.

Their unplanned overnight provided John with a few valuable lessons, and it also became a running joke between the two friends. "For Christmas that year, he sent me a package labeled 'Your New Sleeping Bag.' It was a bandana, of course."

The Possibles Bag

Misadventures such as this were what prompted John Platt to start carrying what he calls his "possibles bag." If you aren't familiar with the Western mountainman of 1960s television, a "possibles bag" is a leather pouch in which the rugged pioneer carried everything that he could possibly need for the day: black powder, flint and steel, a skinning knife—that sort of stuff. The mountain man would never go anywhere without it. In John's case, his possibles bag is a small stuff sack.

"Because I ski and hike and climb, I have all these different packs that I use on different days. I grab my possibles bag and throw it in whatever pack I'm using that day. That way I know I have the basics with me," he says.

The best way to prevent hypothermia is to have enough stuff with you that you can always find a way to warm yourself up, even in bad circumstances. Extra clothes can do it. A Mylar sleeping bag can do it. Starting a fire can do it. A couple of these things combined together can do it best.

"A Mylar blanket would have made all the difference that night in Yosemite. Or even a pack of matches. We were in the trees; we could have started a fire. The Park Service would have been mad at us, but when you're in survival mode, you can break the rules," he says.

The contents of John Platt's "possibles bag."

In John's possibles bag, he carries the necessities to stave off hypothermia. "For fire-starting, I have a candle and a Bic lighter, windproof matches, and a Ziploc baggie filled with cotton balls that have been rubbed in Vaseline. This is awesome fire-starter and it weighs nothing. The cotton balls will burn hot for four to five minutes because of the Vaseline.

"I also have a small collapsible saw that has a six-inch blade. It weighs about four ounces. If you want to be able to start a fire, you need to be able to collect firewood. Using the saw is much easier than trying to break off branches."

Separate from his possibles bag, John also carries weather-protective clothing and shelter: "I have a Mylar bag. Foam pad. Puffy jacket. Heat packs for hands. Here in the mountains, it can snow in the middle of summer," he states. "If you get into trouble in the outdoors, you need two things: You need someone to come get you, and you need to stay alive until they find you. My goal is whenever I go out, I go out with enough stuff to spend the night out. It may not be my happiest night, but I'll be able to get through it."

To avoid hypothermia, your clothes are your first line of shelter (jacket, hat, gloves), but a secondary line (Mylar blanket or sleeping bag or tube-style tent) is critically important if it's raining or severely cold. If you carry enough protective layers and a well-stocked possibles bag, a snowstorm in August is a fun adventure, not a disaster.

And what about the argument that all that extra stuff just weighs down your pack and slows your progress? Take John's advice: "A friend of mine has a saying: 'Fast and light, cold at night.' Going super lightweight is predicated on the idea that when you get into trouble, you can just give up and go home. But that's a poor assumption. Sometimes you can't just walk out."

Lightning Strikes

Another big reason to check the weather forecast is to be prepared for the danger of lightning strikes. According to the National Weather Service, lightning strikes some part of the United States about twenty-five million times each year. Only about 10 percent of people who are stuck will actually die (about fifty per year on average); the other 90 percent become lightning strike survivors who sustain long-term neurological and internal injuries.

The states that have the most lightning-related deaths are Florida, Texas, and Colorado. The higher elevations of Colorado's Rocky Mountains are famous for summer afternoon thunderstorms. At almost every trailhead, signs warn hikers to descend from the mountaintops by noon to avoid lightning. That means if you want to climb one of Colorado's famous fourteeners (peaks that are higher than 14,000 feet), you have to start at the crack of dawn. But strikes can and do happen earlier in the day. In recent years, Colorado has started to experience more lightning in the morning hours.

California's high peaks also see plenty of lightning storms. One of Yosemite National Park's most infamous lightning-related tragedies took place on the park's most iconic chunk of granite, 8,842-foot Half Dome. In late July 1985, five people were struck by lightning on the dome. Two were killed instantly, two were gravely injured with massive internal injuries and third-degree burns, and one suffered only minor injuries. The tragedy could have been prevented but wasn't, thanks to a classic case of hubris. The hikers were a group of young men who saw Half Dome and its formidable sixteen-mile round-trip trail as a macho challenge. The group leader, who had hiked it several times before, had the odd habit of dancing naked on top of the dome—perhaps as a way of teasing the weather gods.

When the group started out in the late morning, the day was fair and warm, but as often happens on summer afternoons, thunder clouds moved in. The men had already completed about eight miles of the hike and approached the base of Half Dome under dark and ominous skies. Despite clearly posted warning signs that told hikers to stay off the dome if lightning threatened, the young men decided to ascend anyway.

The final stretch of trail to Half Dome's summit isn't really a trail. As hikers approach the granite monolith, they climb up and over a massive hump informally called Sub Dome. A granite stairway, consisting of about 600 mostly manmade steps, leads them up the dauntingly steep face. The trail then descends slightly to reach the base of the steel cables that run 200 yards up the back of the dome. Hikers must use two hands and two feet to haul themselves up 440 feet of nearly vertical granite; the pitch is too steep for walking.

Needless to say, this is no place to be if it's raining. Half Dome's slick, wet granite has claimed many hikers' lives. And it's certainly no place to be in a lightning storm.

The young men, fueled by the adrenaline of flirting with the oncoming storm, hauled themselves up the cables right into the storm's vortex. As thunder rocked the skies and torrential rain pelted their bodies, they took shelter in a cave-like rock enclosure known as the "King's Chair." A bolt struck the dome, sending millions of volts of electricity arcing over the wet granite surface and into the rock cave. One of the men died instantly where he sat; another fell 1,800 feet to his death.

Perhaps more extreme than the lightning strike itself was the rescue effort required to save the surviving men. After the storm abated at about 7 p.m., two paramedics happened to be hiking in the area. They administered emergency treatment to the injured while another group of hikers ran down the trail to get help. Soon after midnight, park rangers arrived on Half Dome. They laid out a landing zone on top of the world-famous rock, and a helicopter pilot executed an extremely risky landing by moonlight on top of the granite dome. The injured men were taken to the hospital and the dead bodies were evacuated.

A similar lightning tragedy happened on top of 14,505-foot Mount Whitney in Sequoia National Park. Whitney, the tallest summit in the lower forty-eight United States, attracts hikers from all over the world because of its notable stature and the fact that bagging the peak doesn't require any climbing equipment. Getting there is just a very long walk of twenty-two miles round-trip, which an incredible number of hikers manage to accomplish in one day.

In mid-July 1990, thirteen hikers were celebrating on Whitney's summit when they felt a buzzing sensation in their boots. They looked around and saw each other's hair standing on end. They couldn't hear thunder yet, but they knew a lightning storm was close.

Stay away from summits if clouds are building. You can always climb that peak another day.

On top of Mount Whitney stands a 300-square-foot granite hut with a sheet-metal roof. It was built in 1909 by Smithsonian Institute astronomers, who installed a telescope inside to study Mars. The scientists abandoned the stone structure after a few years, leaving it to thousands of Whitney hikers who have sought shelter from wind, cold, and rain within its walls. But the hut is the last place you want to be in a lightning storm. When lightning strikes caves or small enclosures, there's no place for the electrical charge to release its mighty power; instead that energy gets channeled and intensified inside the space. Not knowing this, the group of thirteen sought shelter in the hut. When a bolt struck, they watched in shock as a large "ball" of electricity bounced from wall to wall. Several of the thirteen hikers were severely burned; one young woman went into cardiac arrest. Fortunately, one member of the group had a two-way radio and was able to call for help. A Forest Service helicopter landed

Half Dome's famous cable ascent is no place to be if a lightning storm is threatening.

near the summit carrying emergency medical personnel and supplies, but it took twelve hours before all the hikers could be evacuated. Everyone except the young woman survived.

Small structures or shelters with exposed openings, like the Mount Whitney Hut, are extremely dangerous in lightning storms.

Quiz question: Where is the safest place for a hiker during a lightning storm?

A: On a high-elevation mountain summit.
B: Inside a small structure with an exposed opening, like a camping shelter or rock overhang.
C: Inside a tent pitched under a tall tree.
D: In a boat on a lake.
E: In a dense grove of trees that are all about the same height—or any other place where there is no obvious high point or tall tree nearby.

Choose answer "E" every time. And while waiting it out in that dense grove of trees, crouch in the "lightning position," balancing on the balls of your feet. No other parts of your body should touch the ground. If you happen to have a climbing rope or a foam sleeping pad, put it under your feet for more insulation. Drop your head down and cover your ears with your hands to protect them from the shockwaves of thunder.

And don't hold on to your metal-framed backpacks or trekking poles, either. They should be at least 100 feet away from you. It's not that the metal attracts lightning; it's that if a bolt strikes, any metal that's on or near your body (belt buckle? jewelry?) makes the damage worse. That goes for aluminum tent poles, too. Your tent is not a good place to be during a thunderstorm, especially if it's pitched high on a ridgeline or underneath a tall tree.

No place is 100 percent safe from a lightning strike, but some places are safer than others. The inside of a modern, well protected building is about as safe as it gets, but that's not usually an option for hikers caught in a storm. (If lightning strikes a building, the plumbing and wiring will conduct the electricity and direct it into the ground. You'll be fine—unless you are touching electrical equipment or cords inside the house.)

Everybody knows that lightning tends to strike the tallest object in a given area. That means mountain summits and high ridges can be deadly. Solitary tall trees can be deadly. Enclosed spaces like caves, huts, alcoves, and rock overhangs can be deadly. Occasionally, lightning will even strike a hiker who is standing alone in a large meadow or clearing. Remember: you don't want to be the tallest object in the vicinity, and you don't want to be *near* the tallest object in the vicinity.

When you're outdoors, any low spot is a good choice in a lightning storm, as long as it isn't a place where rainwater will accumulate. Water is a great conductor, so avoid both small and large bodies of water. People often get struck by lightning on beaches or lakes. Interestingly enough, lightning strikes on rivers are very rare—but that's probably because rivers are often bounded by high cliffs, and lightning will "choose" those high cliffs instead of the river.

Hikers aren't the only lightning victims, of course. Farmers, ranchers, and even people putting out their trash cans in the suburbs have been struck by lightning. Fishermen tend to get struck more often than any other group of outdoor recreationists. Boaters are not far behind. In terms of sports, soccer players are most affected by lightning strikes—although a popular urban myth states that golfers get struck most often.

Here's another misconception worth revealing: most people think that lightning is always accompanied by thunder. Nope. Lightning can strike more than twenty-five miles away from its "parent" thunderstorm. At that kind of distance, you wouldn't hear thunder. Most lightning victims are struck before or after a storm reaches its peak intensity, or in other words, when the storm is just arriving or just leaving. The "edges" of the storm usually produce the most injuries and/or fatalities. That's why you need to find a way to safety immediately when you think a storm is approaching, and why you should always wait at least thirty minutes after the last clap of thunder to leave your shelter and resume hiking or backpacking.

The best way to stay safe from lightning is to avoid it. Check the weather forecast. If it calls for thunderstorms, time your trip to

Small trees like these, which are much lower than the surrounding peaks, are a good place to take shelter during a lightning storm.

avoid them. In the mountains, the general rule is to hike early in the morning as the majority of thunderstorms develop in the afternoon. Set a turnaround time that will get you off the mountaintop before the storm hits. If you hear thunder, turn around immediately. You're only twenty minutes from the summit? Too bad. If you aren't struck by lightning, you will live to bag that peak another day.

Finally, learn how to read the clouds. As you hike, keep your eyes on the sky: if you notice this morning's puffy white clouds growing taller and darker as the day progresses, or if you see a cloud developing into an anvil shape—tall and flat at the top—you're watching a thunderhead develop. Descend from high ridges or peaks immediately. There is no way to outrun a thunderstorm.

Pay attention to the wind, too. Approaching thunderstorms are usually accompanied by a sudden reverse in wind direction, or a noticeable rise in wind speed. Other warning signs: if your

Pay attention to clouds and wind, and learn how to read the skies for approaching storms.

hair begins to stand on end—you start to "feel" the hair on your head or arms; if your skin begins to tingle; if you see a blue halo around any person or object (a phenomenon known as St. Elmo's Fire); or if you hear or feel a "buzzing" in the atmosphere. These are all signs that you're in an extremely highly charged electrical field. You may not yet see lightning, but you need to move fast. It's coming.

To sum up: when lightning is imminent, head for low-lying areas. Get down from mountaintops and ridges. Avoid lone tall trees, wide open areas, and metal objects. Do not seek shelter in caves or alcoves. Stay away from water. Become a smaller target by assuming the lightning position. Squat low on the balls of your feet. Place your hands on your knees or on the back of your neck with your head between your knees. Do not lie down or touch the ground with your hands. Keep as little of your body touching the ground as possible.

Water Hazards

Hikers don't pay enough heed to water. We don't mean drinking it—although that can be a problem, too. We mean drowning in it. The number two cause of death in the outdoors is drowning (number one is falling, according to the National Institutes of Health). Drownings happen to hikers and backpackers most often under three circumstances: 1) when hikers are trying to ford a creek or river; 2) during a flash flood (they're more common than you think); and 3) when someone decides to jump in a river or creek to "cool off." With a little bit of knowledge, many drowning deaths could be prevented.

Make Stream Crossings Safe

Everybody loves to hike near water. Listening to the sound of a creek or river as you walk is one of the great pleasures of the outdoors. But sooner or later your trail may cross that creek or river, and if there isn't a bridge, you need some know-how.

Start with pre-trip planning. Check your maps or ask your local land management agency about possible water crossings on your planned route. Know what you will be up against at the time of year you are traveling. A raging swiftwater crossing in June can be an easy rock-hop in September. In the eastern Sierra, one of the most notoriously difficult stream crossings is on the Convict Creek Trail on the way to Dorothy Lake. The US Forest Service has attempted three times to bridge that crossing, but each time the bridge was wiped out by roaring snowmelt. In early summer, this ford can be deadly, but by late summer, it's only a few inches deep.

The best crossings are the ones in which you don't get your feet wet—in other words, if there's a stable log that you can cross or a series of rocks to step on. At any crossing that looks difficult, take a minute to look upstream and downstream to see if you can find a safer place to cross. You don't have to cross at the exact spot where

Walk upstream and downstream from a trail crossing to look for a well placed log that can serve as a bridge.

the trail crosses. Just 100 feet upriver, there may be a perfectly placed log that will prevent you from getting soaked. If you have to go out of your way to find a safe crossing, so be it.

If your crossing relies on you balancing on a log or rock-hopping, undo your pack's waist strap before you start. That way if you fall into the water, you can remove your pack quickly. A wet, heavy pack could make the difference between swimming and drowning.

Sometimes you have no choice but to ford, or wade right through, a creek or a river. A pair of trekking poles can be incredibly useful in this endeavor. If you don't have poles, find yourself a big stick— about as tall as you are and at least two inches thick.

Here's the key: if the water is running fast, you don't want to cross directly perpendicular to the current. Instead, angle your body upstream. Enter the water facing upstream and create a three-point stance with your two legs and one pole or stick. Place your pole, then angle your feet toward it. This "tripod" will support you against the force of the current. If you keep your body slanted toward upstream, you have much less chance of losing your balance and falling downstream.

It goes without saying, but if you have river sandals or camp shoes, you might want to change into those before you enter the water. Keep your hiking shoes and socks dry for the rest of the day.

If you're traveling with a group of younger or weaker hikers, or if you know you have several crossings to make, consider carrying a light rope of at least 100 feet. The strongest hiker can cross the creek and secure the rope on the far side, then toss it to the others to use as a hand line. If possible, secure it on both sides of the creek.

Flash Floods

In 2005, Rosie and Brett Hackett traveled to idyllic Costa Rica for their honeymoon. With verdant jungles, tropical sunshine, and turquoise waves, the country seemed like the perfect destination for the adventurous newlyweds, who were both backcountry wilderness guides.

A shallow stream like this one can become a raging torrent in a flash flood.

First on their itinerary was the rugged coastline of the Nicoya Peninsula, a surfer's paradise where perfect left-hand waves break on pristine beaches. The couple surfed and lounged on white sand until their skin was sunburned. A daytrip inland—to someplace shady, wet, and cool—was in order.

The couple drove to nearby Mal Pais, a small village renowned for its waterfalls and beaches, and stopped at a trailhead near a cluster of eco-resorts. The muddy parking lot overflowed with cars, and a man waited to take their money.

"A parking attendant wanted two dollars to park our car," Rosie says. She refused. Why pay for parking when it was free to park on the street? But Brett reasoned with his bride—parking cost only two bucks, and besides, the man promised to guard their car while they hiked. Rosie grudgingly handed over the money. The attendant stuffed the bills in his pocket and pointed to an empty parking space.

The newlyweds set out on their hike, following a trail into a steep river canyon where crystal water trickled into shallow, stepped pools.

"There was a rocky trail on one side of the river. On the other side it was wild jungle, super lush with lots of vegetation," Rosie recalls. "It was beautiful, but I was sort of disgruntled the whole time. I couldn't believe we paid for parking."

In the humid afternoon heat, people frolicked in the shimmering pools and lounged on smooth boulders. Rosie and Brett dipped their feet into the water. Wading through the river was more fun than hiking the slippery path along its steep banks, and Rosie's mood brightened. Fluorescent butterflies flickered over the water and monkeys rustled in the foliage. The couple splashed upstream until they reached their destination.

"At the top, there was a massive pool with a huge waterfall," she notes. High above the waterfall, tightly strung ropes zigzagged across the canyon. It was a commercial canopy tour and ropes course. Tourists in helmets and harnesses balanced on the cables, enjoying a bird's-eye view of the roaring cascade and leafy jungle.

"Across the river from us there was a whole family of howler monkeys cruising through the trees and yelling at each other," Rosie says. As the monkeys retreated back into the forest, a cacophony of whoops and howls reverberated behind them. Rosie and Brett glanced back at the children on the boulders—and that's when everything changed.

"They were on rocks that were way above the water, and all of a sudden, the rocks were underwater."

The stream began to churn and boil, turning red with swirling sediment. "The water was rising. It was getting muddy and huge chunks were coming down. As soon as we realized the water was moving, everything happened in five seconds. There was no way to get out of the water."

The marooned children panicked and attempted to leap to safety. "One girl tried to jump on to a rock and it disappeared underwater. She had to swim," Rosie says. "Brett and I ran down and grabbed the other little girl. The two boys were a little older and swam to the opposite side of the river, just barely making it."

Rosie, Brett, and the two girls clung to the slick canyon wall. The flash flood had engulfed the canyon, and from the opposite side of the river, the children's parents looked on in terror. "They were screaming at us, but we couldn't hear a thing because the creek was now a Class 5 rapid," Rosie says. "It was massive, deep brown, and bushes and trees started to come down."

Rosie and Brett began bushwhacking along the river's edge, gathering together other tourists who had been stranded by the flood. "We had no trail on our side, and it was super steep," Rosie recalls. They found four more people, all completely terrified. Their group was now eight, and aside from Rosie and Brett, everyone spoke Spanish.

There was no way to travel down the swollen river canyon, so the group decided to hike uphill to the ropes course above the waterfall. Brett, who spoke a little Spanish, led the way, pushing through the dense undergrowth towards the ridgeline. Rosie corralled the group from the rear.

"We were moving slowly. Everyone kept falling and slipping downhill in the mud. We had to support each other and use all four limbs to pull uphill," Rosie says. "We were all barefoot because everyone who had been caught in the flood lost their stuff."

After several hours, the group finally reached the ridge. By this time it was dark, and strange noises were coming from the shadowy jungle. "I remember hearing all the monkeys and animal sounds," Rosie recalls. "In the Costa Rican jungle, you do not want to be out at night." Costa Rica is home to poison dart frogs, spotted jaguars, and seventeen types of venomous snakes, most of them nocturnal.

"Once we got to the ridge, we could see the lights of the resort," Rosie recalls. She and Brett decided that they would lead the group toward the lights. Around midnight, they finally burst out of the jungle and into the resort parking lot. A large gathering of worried Mal Pais residents—hotel staff, locals, and family members—greeted them. "Everyone was reuniting with their families, hugging each other and crying like they'd almost died," she says.

Rosie and Brett just watched. Since they were strangers here, no one was there to meet them.

"Then all of a sudden we see the guy we paid two dollars to park our car. He was looking for us," Rosie says. "He came running up and hugged us. In the parking attendant's embrace, the shock of the flash flood finally sunk in, and Rosie burst into tears. "We paid him to watch our car and he remembered us. He cared about us."

Brett thrust a $20 tip into the man's hand. As Rosie and Brett, both covered in mud, sank into the spotless seats of their rental car, Brett turned to his wife and said, "See, Babe, that's why you pay for parking."

Flash floods are one of the most deadly forces of nature. They can happen with little or no warning, on perfect blue-sky days, and not just in tropical places like Costa Rica. In the American deserts, flash floods are common occurrences. It's a condition that desert dwellers refer to as "more water than you want in less time than you have." In a flash flood, the rain falls too fast for the soil to absorb it. Or, in the case of a stream canyon like the one Rosie and Brett Hackett were hiking in, the stream goes from a gentle trickle to a menacing wall of water.

Desert canyons that are bone dry most of the year can flood rapidly if there's heavy rainfall upstream.

Places that have extremely low soil moisture and experience frequent thunderstorms tend to be the most affected by flash foods. Desert areas of the Southwest—Arizona, California, New Mexico, and Utah—experience flash floods that are usually brought on by late summer and fall monsoon rains (although floods can occur at any time of the year). Although flash floods occur in almost every state, they are particularly ferocious in desert areas because the desert's arid, sparsely vegetated soil has very little capacity to absorb rainfall. The water doesn't sink in; it just slides. In the desert, even small storms can turn normally dry streambeds into raging torrents of water.

Every year people are killed while walking in a dry creekbed when a thunderstorm happens miles away—sometimes so far away they never even see or hear the storm. Desert washes or creekbeds, which may be bone dry all year long, can become a brown torrent of water if there's heavy rainfall somewhere upstream. Hikers caught in a wash will see the ground go from completely dry to a swiftly moving river in only a few minutes. If they're lucky, they'll be able to scramble to higher ground and watch the spectacle from a safe place. If they're unlucky, they'll be swept away in the torrent.

In September 2015, seven hikers were killed by a flash flood in southern Utah's Zion National Park. Zion, famous for its colorful cliffs and narrow canyons lined with water-worn rock, is Utah's most visited national park. The hikers were negotiating their way through Keyhole Canyon, a narrow slot canyon bounded by vertical walls and carved out by the Virgin River. Thunderstorms were predicted, but no one imagined how intense they would be. More than a half-inch of rain fell in less than an hour, causing the river to rise rapidly. The Park Service immediately called a flash flood warning and closed all of the park's canyons to visitors, but they were unable to get word to people who were already inside the canyons. Keyhole Canyon's steep walls made it impossible for the hikers inside to escape the river of mud and water.

One year earlier, a hiker drowned in a flash flood in the park's famous Zion Canyon Narrows, one of Zion's most popular hikes. Traversing the Narrows requires walking in shallow river water through a winding canyon with steep walls. Local outfitters rent booties, neoprene socks, hiking sticks, and dry suits so that even novices can make the trip. Douglas Yoshi Vo was hiking with a friend when the flood hit, and both men scrambled up to higher ground. They were trapped on cliffs on opposite sides of the river, unable to communicate with each other because of the river's ferocious roar. Rangers estimate that the river was flowing at about forty-six cubic feet per second when the men started their hike, and at the flood's peak, it was flowing at 4,000 cubic feet per second. After about six hours, Vo's companion swam downstream and was able to make it out to safety, but Vo did not.

Grand Canyon National Park has also seen its share of flash floods. In August 1997, twelve hikers were caught in a flash flood in the park's Lower Antelope Canyon that filled the canyon with water up to fifty feet deep. Only one hiker survived. The thunderstorm that generated the flood was more than twenty miles away.

Taos, New Mexico, is another beautiful natural area that is subject to occasional flash floods. In June 2015, a thirteen-year-old Boy Scout was swept away from his backpacking campsite in a flash flood that transformed a small creek, normally one foot deep and three feet wide, into a floodwater twenty-three feet deep and 100 yards wide. The boy was sound asleep when the flood roared through at 4 a.m. Three other Scouts were also swept away in the flood, but they lived.

Death Valley National Park also experiences occasional flash floods. In October 2015, twenty campers and three park rangers spent the night "sheltered in place" in a volcanic crater after being evacuated from Mesquite Springs Campground due to flash flooding. The Grapevine Canyon area of Death Valley received 2.7 inches of rain in five hours, and the ground was already saturated from a previous rainstorm. (Much of Death Valley receives only two inches of rain *per year*.) The deluge left several feet of mud and debris inside the visitors' center at Scotty's Castle, an ornate mansion that is open for guided tours, and destroyed ten miles of park roads.

If you're hiking in a desert canyon, checking the weather forecast is critical. Any time there's rain in the forecast, there's a danger of flash flooding. Be especially cautious from July to September, when severe thunderstorms develop quickly. During these months, be extremely cautious about hiking in streambeds, narrow canyons, washes, and arroyos.

As you hike in a desert canyon, always keep your eyes on what's happening upstream (even if "upstream" is a completely dry wash). Remember that a flash flood can occur even if you have blue sky above you. If you see a flood coming, start climbing. Your margin of safety can be counted in seconds, so head for higher ground immediately. Don't try to cross flowing water or flooded trails if the water is above your knees. Stay put and wait for the water to recede.

Cold Water and Drowning

In movies or on television shows, when actors pretend they're drowning, they wave their arms and call for help. The lifeguard/hero runs down the beach, swims out to the victim, and saves his or her life. But the truth is that a drowning scenario rarely looks anything like this. Drowning people are usually much too busy trying to keep their heads above water or catch their breath or get out of the current that's dragging them away to have time or energy for waving arms and yelling for help. Unfortunately, a drowning person's friends or family may not realize what's happening until it's too late.

There are some signs to watch for, though. If you see a person's mouth is at water level, that's a sign that he or she might be in trouble. If a person's eyes look glassy or distant, that's trouble. If you ask the person if they are okay and they don't answer, that's really big trouble.

Drowning has claimed many victims at the Emerald Pool, an icy basin above one of Yosemite National Park's famous waterfalls, Vernal Fall. The Park Service has posted signs declaring Emerald Pool closed to swimming, but the blue-green waters lure overheated hikers who've just completed the steep trek to the top of Vernal Fall. It's one of Yosemite Valley's most popular trails, but it's more strenuous than a lot of people expect. About 1,500 people make the trek every spring and summer day, gaining 1,000 feet of elevation over a

2.5-mile stretch. When they reach the top of the falls, they feel the urge to peel off their sweaty clothes and cool off—and Emerald Pool entices them, despite the warning signs. If they jump in, the shock of the cold water can throw their bodies into overload.

If you're a strong swimmer, it's easy to think that near-drowning (or drowning) would never happen to you. But here's how it can happen: You're hiking. You're hot and tired. You come to a spot on a river or creek where you impulsively decide to jump in. What you don't realize is that the water is not just cold, it's icy cold, as in 50-degree snowmelt. The shock to your overheated body is extreme. You find yourself involuntarily gasping, and your heart rate and blood pressure rise. You feel a sense of panic and you try to get out of the water. The rocks along the streambanks are slippery, and you can't grab on to them. Your hands and feet are cramping up, and you feel confused and dizzy. As you struggle to exit the water, you're being pulled downstream by the current. Your head bobs under water. You come up and gasp for breath. Your head drops below the surface again.

Even for athletic swimmers, sudden immersion into cold water can cause "cold shock," which translates into gasping, rapid breathing or hyperventilating, panic, and dizziness. If left unchecked, these symptoms lead to water inhalation and drowning. Cold shock often occurs in water temperatures in and around 50 degrees Fahrenheit, and it seems to happen more often if the person's body is overheated when he or she enters the water. The cold shock response can be deadly in itself, especially if the victim gasps while he or she is under water. Of all the people who die in cold water, about 20 percent die in the first two minutes, mostly likely due to cold shock.

What to do? Resist the urge to submerge yourself in cold water, no matter how hot and sweaty you are. Take off your hiking boots, sit down near the water's edge, and stick your feet in, but don't submerge your entire body. If you must wade in, stay close to the shore and don't let the water rise above your knees. Be wary of invisible currents that can knock you over and send you swimming—even if you didn't intend to.

Dealing with Sun and Heat

Katie Zanto is a college professor who teaches outdoor leadership and wilderness education. But in the summer of 1989, she was a sixteen-year-old greenhorn who had zero experience in the backcountry.

That year, Katie's parents signed her up for the month-long excursion with the National Outdoor Leadership School (NOLS). They wanted their teenage daughter to learn about the outdoors, toughen up, and acquire some survival skills. They figured a summer backpacking course would do the job.

Dispatched to the Wind River Wilderness of Wyoming, Katie spent that July hiking and camping with twelve other students and two instructors. "I was in the Rocky Mountains, where there's a lot of granite peaks and lakes," she says. "I was loving it. I was learning how to backpack, rock climb, and fly-fish."

Katie was a fearless hiker who tackled any terrain with gusto. However, the NOLS instructors were concerned with her recklessness. "I was a klutz. I fell a lot and had bruises. I was pretty unaware of my body and the signals it was giving me," she says.

One of the things you learn when backpacking is to be extra careful with your body. "I remember getting feedback from my instructors, and they told me that I needed to take better care of myself," Katie says. Wanting to do well in the course, she tried to be more cautious, but as a carefree teenager, it was hard.

Halfway through the trip, the students decided that a solo hike was the ultimate adventure and begged their instructors to let them venture out un-chaperoned. "Everyone really wanted to have a solo experience," Katie says. "The instructors got together and adjusted our itinerary so we would each have a full twenty-four hours alone in the wilderness."

Each student was assigned a different area that would be their solo arena for the next twenty-four hours. During that time, they were free to explore, as long as they stayed in their respective zones.

"I got this huge basin area, and the instructors told me they'd be back in twenty-four hours and walked away," Katie recalls.

She was left completely alone in a sweeping, grassy meadow surrounded by huge granite peaks. "A solo trip is not about exploration, it's about time by yourself," she says. "I had this entire day to myself, and I thought, *I'm going to hike around nude.*"

For Katie, hiking naked was a revolutionary idea. "I came from a family where we never were naked. We didn't go to hot springs or anything like that. I had never done anything nude," she says. This was her opportunity. After all, she had been told by the instructors to be more aware of her body.

Katie stripped off her clothes and smeared a layer of sunscreen over her naked skin. Wearing nothing but her hiking boots, she strode bare-skinned into the basin. Although the day was warm, the sky was overcast. Cotton clouds hung over the mountains and a slight breeze ruffled the alpine wildflowers blanketing the area.

"I spent the entire day nude. I hiked nude. I frolicked in the woods. It was great. It was freeing," Katie says. "I remember wondering why I'd always been so uncomfortable being naked."

Katie explored every corner of her private wilderness. But as she reveled in her new freedom, the sun was frying her skin. "I wasn't really thinking about the sun. I had swiped on some sunscreen in the morning, but I didn't reapply," she says.

The strength of the sun is deceptive, especially on a cloudy or partially cloudy day. UV rays are amplified by water droplets in the clouds and can burn skin just as easily as on a clear afternoon. Higher elevations and low humidity increase the sun's potency.

That evening, when Katie hiked back down her camp, she realized she might have a problem. "My skin felt really hot and dry," she says. "But I was in the mode of just grinning and bearing it."

Katie camped by a rock outcropping on the edge of her grassy meadow. But the idyllic spot did little to placate her increasing pain. Her skin was on fire, and she slept little that night.

When the NOLS instructors collected their scattered students the next morning, they found Katie in terrible shape. "I was scorched from my neck to my bellybutton. I had burned myself to the point that it hurt to put my backpack on," Katie says.

She was more upset by her blunder than by the pain.

"I had already been told that I needed to take care of myself and be bodily aware," she says. "And I was trying to be more aware! I was hiking nude and learning what that felt like, and I had stumbled into making another mistake."

Over the next few days, Katie's skin blistered and shed like a snake's. For the rest of the trip, a more subdued Katie hiked with care—and covered up her skin. Her burn didn't lead to permanent scarring, but for a few years afterward she wore a reminder of the incident—the imprint of two finger marks across her chest, where she had smeared an extra-thick dollop of sunscreen.

Now that Katie is a backcountry instructor and guide, she always warns her students to protect their skin from the sun. "I talked about this story a lot once I became an instructor," she says. "The sun is powerful and your skin is fragile. You can get sunburned very easily, and it can have serious consequences."

Unless you've been living under a rock, you already know the dangers of the sun. What you might not know is how much those dangers become amplified when you're hiking in higher elevations. The air may be cool in the Rockies or the Sierra Nevada, but the sun is much hotter than it is at the beach. The rules of sunscreen use are simple and finite: Wear sunscreen with a high SPF rating on any exposed skin. For hiking and backpacking, experts recommend you use a water-resistant sunscreen rated at 30 SPF or higher. Put on your sunscreen thirty minutes before you go outdoors so it has time to take effect. And here's the part that everybody forgets: Reapply your sunscreen every two hours. Reapply, reapply, reapply. If you don't think you'll remember, set a timer on your smartphone to remind you.

When you're day-hiking or backpacking, you may be exposed to the sun for eight or twelve hours a day. You'd probably never spend that much time at the beach in the sun. In addition to using sunscreen liberally, cover up your head. Protect your face, scalp, ears, and neck with a broad-brimmed hat. Lots of hikers end up with skin cancers on the tops of their heads or the backs of their necks. Sunburn is bad; skin cancer is much worse. Wearing a hat has the additional

Sun protection is critical for hikers and backpackers. Wear a big hat, sunglasses, sunscreen, and lip balm.

benefit of keeping your brain cooler. It may seem counterintuitive, but a light-colored, lightweight fabric or mesh hat will reduce the amount of heat exposure to your brain.

And even if you wear a big hat, you still need to protect your eyes and lips. Wear high-quality UV-blocking sunglasses to protect your eyes from sun rays and glare, as well as dust and debris on the trail. Cover your lips with balm that has a high SPF rating (many lip balms do not contain any sunscreen at all, so read labels). Reapply your lip balm every time you reapply your sunscreen. Make it a habit.

Hiking in Extreme Heat

Desert temperatures during the summer months can reach upwards of 115 degrees Fahrenheit in the shade, creating brutal conditions for hikers. And yet, a surprising number of people travel to America's deserts in summer. They even visit Death Valley, the hottest place on earth and the driest place in North America, where the air temperature can soar to 134 degrees Fahrenheit. Heat like this may be the most forbidding element your body will ever face. Yet if you take a few precautions, it's possible to enjoy the desert's stark and beautiful scenery even on the hottest days of the year.

Keep in mind four factors when hiking in the desert or anywhere it's extremely hot: timing, water, food, and body temperature.

Timing

When hiking in the desert, timing is everything. Avoid hiking during the hottest hours of the day, typically between 10 a.m. and 4 p.m. Hiking before dawn and after dusk is an excellent way to avoid the heat. Just be sure to carry a lightweight flashlight or headlamp to help guide you in case it gets dark—and keep an eye out for desert creatures like sidewinders, who also wait for the sun to go down. Mornings are a great time to hike in the desert. Get a 5 a.m. start in the Grand Canyon, Zion, or Death Valley and you'll enjoy comfortable temperatures for a few hours plus the chance to see wildlife that you'd never see in the middle of the day.

Timing is also important with regard to rest. In the desert heat, it's important to stop to rest for about ten minutes at least once per hour. Think like a cowboy and find some shade, even if it's just a tiny bit of shade from a boulder. Remove your pack, eat, and drink. Every couple hours, remove your boots to let your feet breathe. Check your feet for hotspots, the precursors to blisters (see Chapter 3: Boots, Blisters, and Foot Care).

Water

While hiking in the arid desert, you can lose as much as two quarts of water per hour. But the human body is only capable of absorbing about one quart of water per hour. Between respiration, sweating, and urination, our bodies have the potential to lose far more water than we can physically replenish. In hot, dry climates, sweat evaporates so quickly that you may not notice how much water you're losing. On hot days, plan on drinking half a liter of water every hour. But that's only half of the equation, and it doesn't work well without the other half. To help your body maintain proper function in extreme heat, you must balance your water intake with electrolytes and food. Sweating causes you to lose electrolytes like sodium, potassium, and magnesium. These electrolytes have an important job; they send signals through your nerves to your muscles. If you don't have enough electrolytes in your system, you can get leg cramps, nausea, and muscle spasms. Or you might just feel really exhausted and crabby and not know why. In more serious cases, your heart can start beating irregularly. Drinking lots of water alone, without food or electrolytes, can exacerbate the problem. Alternating water with electrolyte supplements and salty foods is key to your body's health and energy in hot temperatures. Here's Ann Marie's typical liquid inventory for a five-hour day hike in the desert: one gallon of water, plus one liter of some kind of electrolyte drink. Yes, that sounds like a lot, and she doesn't always drink it all, but she drinks as much as she can. Plus she usually carries an extra pack of a dry electrolyte mix so she can give it to other hikers who are in trouble.

Food

As noted above, you must balance your water consumption with salts and carbohydrates. Our bodies lose salts and electrolytes at an exponential rate while hiking in extreme heat. It is important not only to fuel up with carbohydrates, but also to consume enough salt to balance the amount we are losing. Many of us lose our appetites when our bodies are hot, so it can be hard to force yourself to eat, but do it anyway. Pack along salty foods like pretzels, chips, salted nuts, or jerky. You'll be more inclined to eat salty foods than sweet foods when you're hot, but bring along a few sweet treats, too, like granola bars or trail mix. It's hard to digest food when you're exercising vigorously, so eat and drink small amounts frequently, rather than a lot at one time. Trail mix works well for this because you can just grab a handful every hour.

Body Temperature

What's the bottom line about hiking in the heat? It doesn't matter how much food and water your body receives if it cannot cool itself sufficiently. The only way to stay cool is to avoid the hottest hours of the day, and to take steps to regulate your body temperature. If you're outside in the summer in the backcountry of the Grand Canyon or Zion national parks, you need to take some steps that go beyond eating, drinking, and taking rest breaks in the shade. One good step is to soak yourself with water as often as possible. In addition to the water you're carrying to drink (remember—at least a gallon for a five-hour hike, plus a liter of electrolyte drink), carry a spray bottle filled with water, so you can spritz yourself. Focus on cooling the body's high-temperature areas such as the head, feet, hands, underarms, and groin. Hike "wet" as often as you can. Ann Marie spends a lot of time in Joshua Tree National Park and the Mojave Desert, and if she comes across an oasis, she'll usually stick her head (and her sun hat) directly in the water. Having her hair and hat wet will usually keep her comfortable for at least half an hour.

Heat Stroke

Heat stroke occurs when the body overheats to a temperature that no longer allows the internal organs to cool themselves or properly function. It's very serious and can be fatal. Heat stroke, and its predecessor heat exhaustion, can be prevented by staying well hydrated and keeping your core temperature as close to normal (98.6 F) as possible. We'll repeat ourselves for emphasis: In hot temperatures, you must continually recharge your body's cooling system by drinking sufficient fluids (water and electrolytes), eating, and resting in the shade.

Key to preventing heat stroke is to identify it in its early stages and treat it before the situation becomes dire. Heat stroke begins as heat exhaustion, with symptoms such as profuse sweating, loss of appetite, nausea, dizziness, and possible vomiting. If you think your hiking partner may be suffering from heat exhaustion, get him or her out of the sun, remove backpacks or any excess clothing, and spray him or her with cool water. Try to get him or her to drink cold water. If you can call 911 for medical help, tell the operator that the victim is suffering from heat exhaustion and to bring ice packs.

If heat exhaustion progresses to become heat stroke, the victim may fall into a coma and die in as little as three hours. Heat stroke symptoms include a high body temperature, red or flushed skin and a lack of sweating, rapid heart rate, difficulty breathing, and generally odd behavior including disorientation, hallucinations, and confusion.

8
Navigation: Get Where You Want to Go

The Virtues of Maps

We love the GPS mapping systems on our smart phones. We use GPS when driving around town or walking in an unfamiliar city. And we use GPS to find super-sized nonfat caramel lattes, dog grooming shops, and cobblers who will repair our hiking shoes. But we almost never use GPS devices in the outdoors, and it's not because we're Luddites. It's because we believe that GPS can too easily lead to S.O.S. or worse yet, S.O.L.

A GPS device is a great tool, but it's no substitute for a map. Ann Marie learned to hike and backpack before GPS existed, so she's accustomed to navigating with a map and compass (plus her reading glasses—otherwise she can't read the map or the compass). Terra is twenty years younger, so she thinks compasses are weirdly mysterious and useful only to ancient mariners. But she knows the basics of navigation, and she never goes anywhere in the wilderness without a quality map.

Every search-and-rescue professional we interviewed told us that almost no one understands how to use a compass anymore. But they agreed that good map-reading skills were more important than anything else when it comes to getting around without getting lost. And if you do get lost, a map can show you where you are (via landmarks such as peaks, lakes, ridges, etc.) and what's nearby. If you're off-trail, it can show you how to find your way back to a trail. If you decide not to go the way you originally planned, it can show you alternate routes.

Most importantly, a map can help you determine the easiest way to get to your next destination—without struggling through thick brush, jumping over cliffs, or going up and down a whole bunch of hills you could have easily avoided. A GPS may show you the shortest route to your destination, but it won't necessarily show you the safest or smartest route.

Taking a break to stop and check the map can save you from wrong turns and extra miles.

With a good map, you can determine how far it is to your next destination, and which way you should go. You can pinpoint your exact location by paying attention to landmarks and how fast (or slow) you've been hiking. Way back in our Girl Scout days, this was called "dead reckoning"—multiplying the rate of travel in miles-per-hour by the time spent hiking.

Knowing your rate of travel will help you determine your position, and help you figure out how long it will take to get to your next destination. It will answer the key question, "Will I be able to get there before dark?"

When we carry our heaviest packs, our average hiking speed is about 2.5 miles per hour going uphill, a little faster going downhill or level. (We hike faster if we're day-hiking with only lightweight packs.) So if we're backpacking and Destination Lake is three miles away with a moderate ascent, we know we'll get there in about seventy-five minutes. If we're still hiking two hours later with no lake in sight, we know we screwed up, and we stop to figure it out.

One other reason to love maps: they never need batteries and never experience malfunctions. If Terra drops her map in the lake, she mutters a few bad words (sorry, Mom), then sets her dripping map in the sun to dry. While she waits, she eats raisins and scans the skies for interesting birds or draws a few sketches in her notebook. Not a bad way to spend an hour.

Granted, if the trees are tightly spaced, or if the fog envelops you like you're in a gloomy gothic poem, maps can lose their usefulness. That's when Ann Marie pulls out her compass or checks her altimeter, and Terra sets up her tent and waits until the fog lifts so she can see which way the sun has set (or risen).

For long trips, Ann Marie likes to mark her route on the map with a pen before she leaves. If her trip covers some serious mileage, only a large topographic map can give her a sense of what the terrain is like for a multi-day trip. If the map tells her that she'll have three days in a row with lots of mileage and climbing, then she will plan a rest day on Day 4. Maps have a huge advantage over a GPS screen because they let you "see" a large area. GPS screens can't show you much territory beyond where you are right at this moment.

Once Ann Marie has her route marked on a map, she'll photocopy or scan that map and give it to a friend. If she's hiking solo, she may also leave a copy in her car, so in case she gets in trouble, searchers have a better chance of finding her.

Lisa Whatford, a search-and-rescue expert who searches for missing hikers near Lake Tahoe, California with her dog Beaujet, says, "Hikers will look at their GPS and go, 'Oh, look, this way is shorter.' They have a false sense of security. They rely on technology too much. They're looking at this device instead of looking at the terrain and just having some awareness. A GPS should be a cross-reference, that's all."

"A lot of people get confused by how to read trails," she adds. "Or they don't have a map with them, so if the trail sign lists a destination that's not the exact place you're headed to—maybe it's the next lake above the lake you want—they don't know which way to go. That's why maps matter. You need to know how to orient yourself in the landscape, and not just if you're lost. You need to know where you are in relation to the rest of the wilderness and also the road where you parked your car."

Navigation by Sight

You've heard some people say that they have a good sense of direction. You've heard other people say that they have a terrible sense of direction. Still other people have a poor sense of direction but won't admit it, not even to themselves. They're usually the ones who get lost.

Here's the facts: Anybody can have a good sense of direction if he or she pays attention to their surroundings. Don't just plod along looking at your feet. Don't get so lost in your thoughts that you forget to notice the terrain. Keep scanning around you for landmarks, especially features that are long and linear, like ridges or peaks. Landmarks provide reference points, so even if you're not exactly sure where you are, you know your general location if you can still see Disorientation Peak to the south.

Remember to look behind you, too. Mountains and forests look completely different from different angles. If you're traveling out-and-back to a destination, look behind you occasionally so you know what to expect on your return trip. If you're off-trail, don't be afraid to leave yourself a marker—maybe two sticks crossed over each other or a pile of rocks—to tell you where to find the trail on your way back.

Lisa Whatford says to watch out for what she calls roly-poly terrain, which can disorient hikers. "There's a lot of false peaks in the wilderness, so we get a lot of rescue calls. When it's roly-poly terrain with lots of small hills and valleys, people can get confused by the ups and downs," she says.

"One man was camping by himself and fishing, and he decided he needed to collect some bugs. So he starts looking for bugs on the ground, and he's in roly-poly granite. When he looks up, he doesn't

When hiking off-trail, turn around occasionally so you know what the terrain will look like on your return trip.

know where camp is. And he doesn't know which way to find camp because he's in this undulating terrain that he can't see out of. He was looking down at the ground, so he had no awareness of where he was," Lisa says. "That guy went missing for five days. He was everywhere. He wandered for multiple days before he got found. And he wasn't even hiking, he was just looking around his camp for grasshoppers."

As you hike, look around at your surroundings and pick landmarks so you always know where you are. Figure out which way the lake is. Is it toward the setting sun or the rising sun? Know what that tall, spindly dead tree looks like. Spin around to get a different perspective. Look at what's behind you as well as what's in front of you.

"Children get lost all the time because they stop to pick up a rock or a stick or play at a creek, and they look up and all of a sudden they don't know where they are. You have to keep looking around you, and looking up," Lisa says.

Hiking Off-Trail

Trails are almost always built along the contours where it's easiest for your feet to travel. Trail-builders go to great efforts to construct trails that work with the terrain. Carefully graded switchbacks make it easier to go up a hill. Trails that cut laterally across a mountain slope will get you where you want to go without needless ups and downs.

Trails are great because they usually follow the path of least resistance. Use them whenever you can, and you'll save a lot of time and energy. Never "cut" the switchbacks just to save time. This causes soil erosion and can sometimes confuse other hikers.

With all that said, there are many places where trails don't go—and where you may want to go. Hiking off-trail is a great way to have a true wilderness experience. It's also a common way to get lost or injured. To hike off-trail safely, you need to be skilled with map and compass and skilled at navigating by sight.

Trail Cairns and Blazes

Navigation by sight gets a lot simpler when other people have hiked to your destination before you. Many popular off-trail destinations, like One Thousand Trout Lake and Expansive View Peak, may be surprisingly popular hiking destinations even though an official trail

A small rock cairn like this one can keep you on the right path.

doesn't go there. If enough hikers make the trip, a faint path is created by their footsteps, and that path may be marked with trail cairns or ducks—carefully arranged piles of small rocks.

Cairns are also useful for terrain where it's hard to mark official trails, like where a path traverses granite slabs or crosses a sandy wash where the sand doesn't stay put. Any time you think you've "lost"

the trail, look for these small rock piles. They act as directional signs, marking a "trail" where there is no real trail.

In forested areas, trails or paths may be marked with blazes on tree trunks. Typically they are T- or I-shaped marks that are carved into the tree bark about five feet off the ground, or right around eye level. In some parts of the country, tree blazes may be splashes of white paint.

Compass & Altimeter Basics

Hikers, put down your GPS for a second and take out your topographic map, compass, and/or altimeter. Place the map on the ground and prepare to orient it to the real world. Set the compass on top of the map and orient it to the map's magnetic north declination line (that "N" line is usually printed in a corner of the map). Twist the map and compass together until the north-pointing needle is lined up with either 360 or zero degrees on the compass. Now your map is properly aligned. In most cases, you will be able to spot landmarks around you, such as prominent mountaintops, so take a few sightings on those. Write down their bearings and draw their lines on the map. Where those lines cross is where you are.

If you're in the middle of low-lying clouds or dense rainfall and the mountains are obscured, check your altimeter as well as your compass. If your altimeter says you're at 8,200 feet and you know that you are following Swiftwater Creek, scan the elevation lines on the map near Swiftwater Creek until you find the 8,200 line, and you'll be able to pinpoint your position.

Map Details Matter

If you learn how to read a map properly and always carry one with you, you'll have all the information you ever need to get "unlost." If you carry a compass AND a topographic map, and if you know how to use them, you just increased your insurance policy ten-fold. But there's an important caveat: The quality of your map is critical. Ideally you always want a map that has forty-foot contour intervals, so you're getting as much detail as possible about the area you're traveling in.

Erica Nelson can tell you what can happen when you carry a map that doesn't show enough detail. It cost her six unplanned days and nights in the Alaskan wilderness.

When Erica was twenty-three, she moved to Alaska on a whim. She got a job in Healy, right outside of Denali National Park, working as a housekeeper at a wilderness lodge. There, she met twenty-five-year-old Abby Flantz, another adventurous young woman. When the two friends weren't working, they explored Healy and its surrounding trails. Craving a bigger adventure, the pair planned a short backpacking excursion in Denali.

The hike was supposed to be a twenty-mile jaunt that meandered along the Savage River and then followed Dry Creek back to Healy. The women planned to ride the bus to Mile 15 on the Denali Park Road, then walk back to Healy in less than two days. There was no trail, but the women had a map and were confident they could navigate through the backcountry, even though neither had backpacked much before.

Erica and Abby borrowed a tent, and stuffed their packs with two peanut butter sandwiches, two apples, and five granola bars.

"I thought, we are only going to be gone for one night, so what's the big deal?" Erica says. "I bought a kids' compass from the Denali Visitor Center. For a knife, I threw a box-cutter into my backpack." Finally, they grabbed two bottles of water from the store before heading for Denali.

It was a Thursday in early June. Snowfields blanketed the Alaskan high country and the rivers were engorged with spring snowmelt. The women enjoyed easy hiking on a popular, well-worn route for the first couple of miles. When they reached the rushing waters of the Savage River, they forded carefully. From that point on, there was no trail. Erica and Abby bushwhacked along the banks, making their way downriver through a dense thicket of alders and willows.

"We just started going, and were having a great time," Erica says. "Here and there, we would stop and check the map."

They hiked and explored throughout the long June day, and then as the Alaskan summer sun faded, they set up camp beside the river and fell asleep.

The next morning Erica and Abby packed up their tent and set off toward Healy. They kept following the river, stopping every once in a while to check on their navigation. Unfortunately, their large-scale map covered all of Denali National Park, and it didn't show any detail of the small region where they were hiking. The women felt a trickle of doubt as they noticed that the terrain around them didn't quite match the map, but they assumed the hike was just taking longer than expected because they were bushwhacking off-trail.

"We just kept going and going," Erica says. "We wanted to believe that we knew where we were. So we convinced ourselves of where we were on the map."

Erica and Abby hiked for nearly eleven hours on Friday, heading far off course. They didn't realize that the mighty Teklanika River had joined the Savage River, and at the rivers' confluence, they had taken a wrong turn and were now following the Teklanika. The women weren't heading back to Healy; they were wandering deeper into the remote wilds of Denali.

Their hike was dragging on, but Erica and Abby didn't worry much. It was only Friday, and they didn't have to work until Saturday. They thought they had plenty of time to finish the journey.

"We are both optimistic people. We always think everything will be okay," Erica says.

The balmy afternoon turned to evening, and then it was night. Erica and Abby trekked onward, then finally stopped and made camp. They had eaten their peanut butter sandwiches and run out of water long ago.

"We didn't have a water purification system, so we started drinking out of the river," Erica says. The risks of drinking unfiltered water didn't dampen the women's high spirits. They knocked their water bottles together and said, "Cheers to giardia!"

On Saturday morning, Erica and Abby rose early and scuttled along. They had to work that afternoon. Surely their hike would end soon, they thought. It was only twenty miles and they'd already been hiking for two days. But when afternoon rolled around, the girls missed their shift at the hotel.

Back in Healy, when neither woman showed up for work, their boss at the lodge called 911. A search-and-rescue team was dispatched immediately, but Erica and Abby hadn't told anyone where they were going, or even that they were going backpacking. After some phone calls, searchers discovered that the women had applied for a wilderness permit at the Denali Ranger Station. The permit listed a section number corresponding to the area where the women planned to camp. A helicopter was sent to comb the area along the Savage River, but the women were nowhere to be found.

By Sunday, fear and worry began to nag at Erica and Abby. "We had no idea that anyone was looking for us," Erica recalls. "We just thought we would be in so much trouble for missing work. The stress was finally getting to us."

They were drained, hungry, and sure they'd lost their jobs. Abby began to feel physically ill.

"We still hadn't made any progress, and Abby freaked out," Erica says. "She turned pale and couldn't walk anymore. She was really dehydrated."

Erica gave Abby a pep talk and persuaded her that they weren't lost, merely out for a lengthy stroll. Somehow she convinced Abby to keep moving. The women went into survival mode. They captured rain for drinking water and used Erica's box-cutter to shred fabric for bandaging their legs, which were cut and bleeding from bushwhacking. They rationed the last granola bar that Erica had in her backpack.

"We would set goals, like if we made it to a ridge we would each eat a crumb of the granola bar," Erica says.

Through it all, the women continued to believe that they were still following the Dry Creek drainage to Healy. Whenever one of the women felt doubts, the other always reassured her that they had simply underestimated the terrain.

"It was just back and forth overly positive thinking," Erica states.

Five days had passed since the women had gone missing. More than 100 people were searching for Erica and Abby. Five planes and helicopters were deployed to search a 100-mile area. But with no sign of the women, the search-and-rescue operation was morphing into a recovery mission. The searchers started looking for bodies.

"They thought we were dead because the river flow was so high, the grizzly bears were coming out of hibernation, and we didn't have the gear or food to stay more than one night. Everybody thought we were goners," Erica says.

By Wednesday, the women had been out hiking for six days. It had been raining for the last two days, all of their gear was wet, and they were tired, hungry, and frustrated. Erica and Abby made a drastic decision to leave the water's edge and hike west, in the direction they believed the highway was located.

"We knew we couldn't stay one more night. We had nothing. We were exhausted and soaked. I think hypothermia would have set in that night. So we just bee-lined it west. Once we left the river, we ended up having to drink out of mud puddles," Erica recalls.

As they climbed over a ridge and into a meadow, Erica noticed two towers jutting through low clouds on the horizon. She took out her cell phone, which hadn't had service all week, and turned it on. A faint signal appeared on the screen.

Erica immediately called her mother's number. At the moment her phone rang, Erica's mother was sitting at the Denali Ranger Station being told that her daughter had likely perished.

Erica told the Denali rangers where she thought they were, in the Dry Creek drainage. A helicopter was immediately dispatched to rescue them. But hours later, the women were still sitting in the meadow and there was no sign of a helicopter. Erica called again.

"They said, 'Where are you? We've been searching all over for you,'" Erica says. "That's when everyone, including us, realized that we had wandered way off course."

Erica texted information to the searchers using her compass and photos of the surrounding landscape. Eventually, the pilot was able to zero in on the women's location using Erica's texts and transmission information from the cell tower. Erica and Abby were more than forty miles away from where they believed they were. Soon they were in the helicopter heading back to the ranger station.

Of course the women were embarrassed about how wrong they had been in their navigation. But in the end, getting lost and getting found wound up shaping Erica's future. A few months after being rescued, Erica enrolled in the National Outdoor Leadership School (NOLS) and graduated as a backcountry guide.

Now when Erica shares her story with her NOLS students, she emphasizes the importance of knowing critical skills and being prepared. "For me, this was a second chance. I find it very important to educate people on the basics of hiking—to tell someone where you are going, how to read a map, and how to pack a bag and be prepared," Erica says.

Even Maps Aren't Perfect

As much as we love maps, we never trust our topo map completely, especially for off-trail travel. A twenty-foot cliff may not show up within forty-foot contour intervals, and a twenty-foot cliff can kill you. If you're hiking on established trails, you can trust your map 99.9 percent of the time. But if you hike off-trail, you have to rely on your map-reading skills to plan your route, and then you have to adjust your plan based on what your eyes tell you. And sometimes that means you have to turn around and go back, as painful as that may be. Scout Sorcic tells a story about that.

In June 2013, Scout went backpacking with her college outdoor leadership class in the canyons of southeast Utah, near Canyonlands National Park. The grueling, twenty-one-day trip through the desert was designed to test the students' backcountry skills. Scout, who grew up in Colorado's Rocky Mountains, was unaccustomed to desert hiking.

"There was a lot of cacti and very little water," Scout says. "Just big, red rock canyons and desert terrain."

Each day, the instructors gave their students a mission to accomplish in the backcountry. They were challenged with a variety of survival skills from rock climbing to off-trail navigation. In the last week of the journey, Scout and her fellow students hiked without their instructors. Their assignment was to locate a water source and find a way out of the wilderness.

"We had to plan our own route through a canyon, which is an amazing and authentic experience, but definitely has its challenges," Scout says.

Scout's group took an obscure trail, trekking deep into the desert. The students discovered a water pump at an abandoned ranger station. Grateful to have found water in the parched landscape, they filled their dromedary bags. Each held seventeen pounds of water, or about eight liters.

Their backpacks weighed down with water, the students marched along the trail, happy to have nearly finished their exhausting expedition. "We were going to get out of there, and we were all looking forward to a hot shower and a cold drink," Scout remembers. "We'd been drinking lukewarm water with tadpoles in it and backpacking for three weeks. We were ready for a shower."

The group strategized an off-trail route to their pick-up point, which was located on the far side of Mule Canyon. Examining their topo map, they noticed a drainage that looked like a steep yet clear-cut way to hike from where they were to the top of Mule Canyon. There, the students could camp for the night and descend into the canyon the next day.

"The route seemed fairly straightforward on the map," Scout says, "but as soon as we dropped into it, we realized the drainage was full of gambel oak." Gambel oak is a native Utah tree that grows in nearly impenetrable thickets. "The oak was dense, leafy, thorny, and horrible," Scout says. "Our group called it 'recreational bushwhacking' because we were actually opting to do this." It took the students over six strenuous hours to accomplish the two-mile trek to their designated campsite.

When the group finally staggered onto the ridge, they saw the entire area was covered in cacti and cryptobiotic soil, a live desert topsoil that requires thousands of years to grow.

"The soil is raised, gray, and looks three-dimensional," Scout says. "The darker gray it is, the older it is, and the soil is a stark contrast to the red sand underneath." Hikers who come across cryptobiotic soil in the desert are required to do the "crypto-tiptoe," that is, walk lightly and try not to destroy the fragile ecosystem.

To avoid the delicate soil, the students camped in a nearby bramble pile. They flattened the prickly bushes as best they could and slept tightly together, trying not to move. "One girl rolled over in her sleep and got a cactus stuck in her face," Scout says.

Early the next morning, the students awoke and walked down the ridge to scout out their proposed route through Mule Canyon. To their frustration, they discovered that the route they'd seen on the map was sheer and impassable. "We had two options. We could sit there and spend the rest of our days at the top of the canyon, or we could go back the way we came in," Scout says. "So we turned around, and hiked back up the two miles and six hours of gambel oak."

Scout says her biggest lesson from that trip was learning that when traveling off-trail, a map won't always give her a complete picture of every obstacle she might encounter.

"If you are going off-trail, you need to be prepared for tough terrain. The map can't tell you what the vegetation will be like," Scout says.

Traveling off-trail is a great way to test your navigation skills, but it often presents unexpected problems. And it can happen in the mountains just as easily as the desert. Ann Marie once took a day hike in Desolation Wilderness, not far from her house. It was a hike she had done many times before, but this time when she reached the large lake that was her destination, it was still early in the day and she didn't need to hurry back. She thought, "I wonder if I can walk all the way around that lake?" This particular lake is huge—more than 60,000 surface acres—so she figured it might take her a couple of hours, but she had time.

According to her topographic map, there was no trail on the lake's west side, but there weren't any steep cliffs coming straight down into the lake, either. From her position on the lake's east side, it seemed perfectly reasonable to walk all the way around it, so off she went. Everything went fine until she got almost exactly halfway around. Suddenly there were giant blocky boulders, ranging in size from ten to fifteen feet, obliterating the shoreline. Ann Marie was able to boulder-hop along their jagged, uneven tops, but her foot placement was tricky and the going was very slow. It was much more difficult for her ninety-pound golden retriever, who was dutifully following her, probably wondering when they were going to get back on a trail.

She checked the map again. It showed exactly nothing. According to her map, this west side of the lake looked exactly like the east side, which had a lovely, level trail skirting along its edge.

What to do—keep slogging along or turn back? Ann Marie kept thinking that this blocky stretch would end shortly. Maybe she was just walking through a massive rock slide, a common occurrence in the Sierra. She continued on, but the boulders did not end. Finally, fearing that her dog might slip and fall, she strapped her day-pack on to her head and waded into the ice-cold lake. Her dog followed, happy to be off that boulder field. He dog-paddled and she waded about ten feet from shore until they reached the end of the boulder field, which turned out to be another three-quarters of a mile.

Lesson learned? If there isn't a trail built in a certain area, there might be a good reason. Trail builders construct trails where the topography is friendly for building trails. They're following the path of least resistance, and you should, too.

Another lesson learned? For off-trail travel, topo maps are lifesavers, but you still have to rely on your eyes and make good decisions as you go. Cliff faces can be solid or loose. Snow can be hard in the mornings and soft in the afternoons. Brush thickets can be carved with deer trails or impenetrable. Blocky boulders can make a route impassible even if they aren't big enough to appear on a topo map. Alter your route accordingly.

Group Travel & Navigation

It's surprising how many hikers get lost when they're hiking with a group. It may be because they don't pay much attention to where they're going—they assume the leader has everything figured out. But what if he or she doesn't? Never blindly trust your leader. Note all landmarks and trail junctions as if you were leading the group. Evaluate what you're seeing and how long you've been hiking, and compare that to what you know about your planned hike. Check

Even a small day pack is large enough to carry basic survival supplies that can sustain you if you become lost.

the map when you take rest breaks. If you don't like the route you're taking or the direction you're heading, speak up. Take charge of your own hike, even if you're with a group.

And make sure everybody stays together. If anyone needs to split off from the group for any reason, make sure they have a trail map and know how to read it. Otherwise, don't let anyone go alone.

If You Get Lost

There's a standard piece of advice for people who get lost, and it's proven to be very effective: stay put. Find a tree or a big rock or some other noticeable landmark, preferably right along a trail, and don't move. A lost person is much easier to find if they stay in one place.

While you're staying put, whistle or shout loudly at regular intervals (whistling is more effective). Focus on keeping yourself warm and dry while you wait to be found. Ideally, you prepared adequately

Take a moment to sit down and gather your thoughts, and you may figure out a way to get "unlost."

for your hike, and you have a few basic survival supplies in your pack: a jacket, hat, Mylar sleeping bag, lighter, water-purification device, extra food, a flashlight or headlamp, and a decent knife. If you start to feel cold sitting still, do jumping jacks or run laps around a tree, but don't let your clothes get sweaty and wet.

Getting lost is not a leading cause of death in the outdoors; hypothermia is. Keep your body warm and dry. If you have food or water, eat or drink. If you give your brain and body water and glucose, you may find yourself able to think more clearly, which can help you get "unlost."

Panic vs. Reason

In 1981, twenty-one-year-old John Kleinfelter landed a dream job with the California Department of Fish and Game restoring native golden trout to the Little Kern River. This mountainous region of the

Southern Sierra is heavily forested with thick underbrush, towering trees, and an abundance of alpine streams. John and his fellow biologists spent their days surveying streams in the area and their nights camped in the wilderness. Their food and supplies were packed in by horses, mules, or sometimes llamas.

John was assigned to work under lead biologist Dan Christenson. "His nickname was Captain Midnight," John says. The diligent biologist was infamous among his peers for working on the river till dark. "The first night I worked with him, we got back to camp right around dark. Everyone else was teasing me and saying, 'Welcome to working with Dan; this is what he does.'"

The next evening, John was surveying golden trout in a small stream many miles from camp with Dan, Dan's wife, and an ornery llama named Bentley, who was carrying the equipment.

"Everyone else had already gone to camp, but we were still working along the creek," John says. "I was thinking, it's 5 p.m. and we still have a few miles to go... Okay now it's 6 p.m. ...The hours kept passing and I thought, 'When are we just going to say enough?'"

Captain Midnight ignored the declining light and continued to work. The sun was barely peeking over the ridge, the last rays of light disappearing, when he finally looked up from his work and announced, "Okay, let's go to camp."

The group started off, moving slowly because of Bentley, who had never been trained to carry equipment. When they reached a stream crossing, Bentley refused to hike any farther. The group sat on the riverbank, letting the llama rest. Finally, Dan told John to go ahead and walk to camp alone. He and his wife would follow shortly with Bentley.

John didn't know the way back to camp, but Dan instructed him to follow the trail until he reached Rifle Creek. From there, he recalls, the biologists' camp was only a few hundred yards upstream.

John took off, hurrying through the shadowy forest toward Rifle Creek. But as it grew darker, staying on the trail through the dense forest grew difficult. "It got to the point where it was completely dark," John says. "I didn't have a map, there was no moon, and I didn't have a flashlight."

John struggled to control his growing anxiety. "There were no landmarks," he says. "It was pitch black and I couldn't see a thing. But I could feel the trail underneath my feet."

By sense of touch, he inched along the path. "I was thinking, here I am all alone, and I'm not sure where I'm going," John says. "What I remember very distinctly was the feeling of overwhelming fear. I was scared, and the fear factor was intense."

He crept through the dark until suddenly, the path ended in a T-junction. The trail went right or left, but not straight. John had no idea which direction to go. He froze, his heart thundering in his chest, unable to recall Dan's directions.

"The funny thing about fear is that it takes over and overcomes everything," John says. "I was on the verge of tears and didn't know what to do, so I sat down in the middle of the trail." As he tried to calm his ragged nerves, he wondered if he'd missed a junction, or maybe passed Rifle Creek. How far could he be from camp?

He sat on the trail in the pitch black for nearly half an hour, puzzling over what to do.

"What happened next was pretty amazing," John recalls. "The fear just left. I started to calm down and my fear was replaced by reason."

As he grew calmer, he realized he could faintly hear the sound of rushing water. He also discerned that the trail to the left sloped downhill, while the trail to the right climbed higher into the forest. "Then I remembered the directions Dan told me," John says. "He said 'when you get to Rifle Creek, go upstream.' I realized that I knew what to do."

John stood up and took the left trail, his ears leading him to Rifle Creek. Groping through the dark, he followed it upriver. "An hour later, I saw lights and heard voices in the distance. I'd made it back to camp," he says.

For John, the take-home message that day was about not letting fear overtake reasoning. If you think you are lost, anxiety or even panic can set in. The best thing to do is stop and wait until you can think clearly again. "Don't make decisions when you're fueled by fear," John says. "When you get lost, or when fear takes over, sit down and let it pass. If you wait long enough, you will think reasonably again."

About the Authors

Ann Marie Brown

Ann Marie Brown is the author of thirteen hiking guidebooks and hundreds of articles about travel and outdoor recreation. Her work has appeared in *Sunset*, *VIA*, *Backpacker*, *Smithsonian*, and many other magazines. She spends her summers backpacking and hiking throughout the West and her winters teaching journalism and travel writing classes. Her home base is Lake Tahoe, California.

Terra Breeden

Terra Breeden is a journalist who divides her time between exploring the mountains surrounding her Lake Tahoe home and her trips
to Southeast Asia and Central and South America. Her day job is
writing for *Tahoe Quarterly* magazine and *Forbes Travel Guide*, but
her passions are fly-fishing and backpacking in the Sierra Nevada
Mountains.